THE
OFFICIAL
HOLLYWOOD
HANDBOOK

THE OFFICIAL

Hollywood Handbook

By John Blumenthal

*Photography and Illustrations
by George Kenton*

A WALLABY BOOK
PUBLISHED BY SIMON & SCHUSTER, INC.
NEW YORK

Published by Wallaby Books
A Division of Simon & Schuster, Inc.
Simon & Schuster Building
Rockefeller Center
1230 Avenue of the Americas
New York, New York 10020
WALLABY and colophon are registered trademarks of
Simon & Schuster, Inc.

Book design: H. Roberts Design

10 9 8 7 6 5 4 3 2 1
Manufactured in the United States of America
ISBN: 0-671-49713-8

☆ ☆

Acknowledgments

Literally millions of people assisted directly and indirectly in the development of *The Official Hollywood Handbook*, but since this isn't the Academy Awards, I'll refrain from naming each and every one of them. Of course, I'd like to thank my producers, Dr. and Mrs. Fritz Blumenthal; my agent, Lynn Seligman; my cinematographer, George Kenton; and my editor, Gene Brissie.

Many sincere thanks are also owed to Ingrid van Eckert, G. Barry Golson, Chuck Thegze, and Jeff and Marcie Brawer for their unflagging encouragement and support. Mark Burley, Kathy Kenton, Michael Brock, Penny Santiago, Ron Neter, Mona Neter, Sue Brock, Michael Berry, and Judy Boasberg were also extremely helpful in a variety of ways.

☆ ☆

Contents

Hol-ly-wood (hol'-ē-wŏod) *n.* 1. A district of Los Angeles, California; center of the American motion-picture industry. 2. The U. S. motion-picture industry or the somewhat meretriciously glamourous atmosphere often attributed to it.

☆ ☆

Introduction

To most of us Hollywood is that sun-drenched, palm-lined paradise where the beautiful people get together to make motion pictures. We envision Rolls-Royces and Bentleys crowding the curbs of Rodeo Drive, moguls and agents dickering over gross points in the cushioned comfort of the Polo Lounge, gorgeous starlets lolling about heart-shaped swimming pools for weeks on end. Everyone is tan. Everyone is rich. Everyone drives a Mercedes.

So much for the hype (see Hype: Part One, page 37). Behind the well-crafted facade of glitz and glamour, the *real* Hollywood actually falls somewhere between *Lost Horizon* and *The Asphalt Jungle*. It is a rough town, especially for the tens of thousands of ambitious newcomers who still come in droves to knock on the same doors and claw up the same slippery ladder every year. Film school diplomas in hand, they all discover the hard way that Hollywood unrolls the red carpet for no one. To make it in Hollywood, to even survive, you have to play the game. It is relatively easy once you know how, but learning the rules, the do's and don'ts, is fundamental.

Granted, bookstore racks are crammed with how-to manuals on the nuances of screenwriting, acting, and directing, and film school rosters are overcrowded with students aspiring to careers in filmmaking. But ask yourself this: Did Sam Goldwyn need a degree in producing to make it in Hollywood? Did John Ford study German Expressionist Cinema to get his first directing deal? Did David O. Selznick attend NYU film school? Of course not. That is not to say that course study and text material are not helpful in developing skills, but in Hollywood skill is hardly a requirement. Infinitely more important is knowing how to hustle Hollywood-style, how to speak the language and how to make it *appear* as if you know what you're doing. That is what this book will endeavor to teach you. You will learn, for example, how to drop names effectively, how to converse like a producer, how to get your name in the trades, what kind of car to drive, where to be seen, how to be truly laid-back and casual, how to select a status address, how to interpret agentese, what to wear, when to take the Mercedes and when to take the Rolls, how to identify hype, where to take a meeting, how to make a deal, how to get ahead through nepotism, hype, chutzpah and the casting couch and, in the hallowed tradition of Sammy Glick, how to manipulate others for personal gain.

Yes, fans, everything is here in living black and white, your indispensable guide to Hollywood success. Soon (we hope) to be a major motion picture.

PART ONE

How to Make It in Hollywood

(LA Visitors Bureau)

☆ ☆

The Initiation Process

There is nothing Hollywood despises more than a true success. Particularly a young, arrogant success. Like any highly competitive community in which everyone is vying for the same trophy, Hollywood is rife with envy. But success means clout, and though everyone will hate your guts for having gnawed your way to the top, they will invariably swallow their pride and become as ingratiating as good taste permits. For this reason alone, success in Hollywood is worth the effort.

However, while you are scratching your way up the ladder, no one will be rooting for you. They will do their utmost to make it *appear* as if they're rooting for you, but deep down they will be ardently hoping that you fall on your face. Hollywood loves a failure.

Keep those factors in mind and you'll be way ahead in understanding what makes Hollywood tick.

☆

How Not to Make It in Hollywood—
A Typical Scenario

Imagine that you have just arrived in Hollywood, fresh out of a midwestern liberal-arts college, where you received high grades and solid encouragement during four years of taking screenwriting classes. Your dream is to become a famous screenwriter. You see yourself neck-deep in steaming Jacuzzi water with directors like

Hollywood Boulevard's Walk of Fame still has a few empty stars waiting for names.

Steven Spielberg and George Lucas, discussing the character development and denoument of your latest script, trying to decide whether Warren Beatty or Jack Nicholson will do your dialogue justice. You envision yourself humbly accepting the Academy Award for best screenplay; you hear bellboys crooning out your name as you sit discussing gross points with your agent in the Polo Lounge, casually sipping Perrier with lime, while six-figure numbers trip over your tongue like Chiclets; you see yourself raking in big bucks every time you switch on your word processor.

You have driven to Hollywood in your somewhat beat-up 1978 Honda Civic, a graduation gift from your parents. You have no agent. You have no worthwhile contacts. You have no credits. You have no serious money, and your last name is not Zanuck, Stark, or Yablans. All you have is ambition and talent.

Good luck, buddy. You may not realize it yet, but you haven't even parked and already you've made some glaring errors. They are the following:

1. You have no agent.
2. You have no contacts.
3. You have no serious money.
4. You have no credits.
5. Your last name isn't Zanuck, Stark, or Yablans.
6. You are driving the wrong car.
7. You are operating under the collegiate illusion that ambition and talent are sufficient grounds for success.

As a result of this typical naiveté, you will be compelled to submit to Hollywood's "Initiation Process," otherwise known as "The Runaround." Hollywood will encourage you, flatter you, even buy you lunch, but no one will actually purchase your material. Your agent, once you land one, will take you to the Polo Lounge and promise you riches beyond your wildest dreams, then disappear suddenly from the face of the earth. Your phone calls will go unreturned for up to three weeks at a time, and whenever you attempt to get in touch with someone you will be told that "he's in a meeting." You will be informed time and again that Hollywood is looking earnestly for fresh, new talent, but no one will be offering you work. Everyone will always claim to be "high," on your projects, but no one will put his money where his mouth is.

"The Runaround" will last about three years.

Eventually, of course, you will catch on to the error of your ways. You will realize that Hollywood is a game and that you'd better start playing. You will begin to develop contacts and use them to make more contacts. You will casually tell others that you own a new Mercedes 380SL, that you are represented by ICM, and that you are a close personal friend of Ray Stark. You will learn to be seen at the right places and to use flattery for personal gain. You will only go to parties populated by those who can further your career. Your scripts will gradually become more commercial and proportionately less coherent. You will still have no credits, but you will say that you've got a deal pending at (choose one) Paramount, Fox, Columbia, Orion, Warner's, MGM/UA, Universal.

What this means is that you have found the ladder. Now all you have to do is start climbing.

HOLLYWOOD 101:
☆☆☆ PRELIMINARY COURSE MATERIAL ☆☆☆

Although Hollywood has been portrayed in numerous books and movies, only a few tell the true story. The following are a few of the more accurate appraisals.

Books

1. *The Disenchanted* by Budd Schulberg. A perceptive account of the way Hollywood treats writers, based loosely on the unhappy experiences of F. Scott Fitzgerald.

2. *Day of the Locust* by Nathanael West. West's characters represent the residue of Hollywood life once the dream has evaporated.

3. *What Makes Sammy Run?* by Budd Schulberg. A portrait of Sammy Glick, the man who climbed the Hollywood ladder by using other people as the rungs. Oddly enough, many present-day Hollywood movers and shakers consider Glick a role model, which was hardly the author's intention.

Movies

1. *Sunset Boulevard.* Young William Holden's portrayal of a down-and-out writer and Gloria Swanson's rendition of a washed-up actress are as accurate now as they were in the late forties when the film was made.

2. *S.O.B.* A biting satire of Hollywood, based loosely on the experiences of director Blake Edwards.

3. *A Star Is Born.* Although Vicki Lester's rise to stardom is mostly fantasy, Norman Maine's deterioration is fairly realistic.

☆ ☆

Paths of Glory

"You've got to take the bull between your teeth."
—*Sam Goldwyn*

Basically, there are eight proven ways of making it in Hollywood. No one much cares *how* you get to the top so long as you get there and are able to stay there. There is, for example, no stigma attached to making it through well-placed relatives or by simply having enough money to purchase your very own film studio. On the contrary, these are considered admirable methods. In Hollywood anything goes.

No matter how you try to make it—be it through chutzpah or hype—luck plays a very important role in the overall process. Even though one certainly cannot orchestrate one's fortune, one can be shrewd and clever enough to be at the right place at the right time often enough to improve the odds. This, of course, requires knowing where the right places are and when the right time is, hardly a simple task in a town as flaky and unpredictable as Hollywood.

Finally, it should be noted that talent plays a decidedly back-seat role in the Hollywood success game. The equation goes something like this: if you are successful, you are by rights talented. If you are not successful, you are by rights a hack.

The following is a comprehensive discussion of the eight methods for making it in Hollywood, beginning with the simplest and concluding with the most agonizing.

☆

Nepotism or "Hello There, Uncle Zanuck . . ."

Favoring one's kinfolk may be common practice throughout the world, but in Hollywood it runs rampant and is widely accepted as standard procedure. Children born in Tinseltown learn very quickly that the industry is where it's at. If Daddy or Mommy happens to be a studio exec, agent, star, director, or producer, the sibling has it made from birth. It is not unusual (in-deed, it is the norm) for the twenty-one-year-old daughter of a mogul to suddenly find herself in the position of Director of Creative Development at her father's production company. Sometimes he will be discreet and set her up for a summer internship before bestowing full honors. At other times he will dispense with this charade and carry her right to the pinnacle.

The Fonda Family (Globe)

Naturally, those who have clawed their way up from the story department will find this procedure somewhat disconcerting. Privately, they will make a lot of sarcastic noises, but publicly they will be compelled to grin and bear it.

Of course, on most occasions, nepotism is less blatant. A father will simply encourage his child, but desist with direct, obvious handouts. He will insist that the little brat make it on his or her own without his aid or assistance. Although this may appear somewhat cruel, it is not—all the ambitious offspring need do is mention

Daddy's illustrious name a few times and the doors will crash open with the same ferocity with which they slam shut in the faces of those less fortunate. Then, when the kid makes it big in less than a month, Pop can congratulate himself for having sired a child able and canny enough to make it on his or her own wits.

As mentioned earlier, nepotism in Hollywood is an acceptable tradition taken for granted by most people in the industry. What does tend to rankle Hollywood is when the young success appears on talk shows and tells the host, between sincere sobs, that his or her famous name was more of a drawback than a boost. You've probably heard this spiel before: "No, Merv, the fact is, I had to overcome my famous name (sob). . . . People immediately expected more of me (sob). . . . It made it much more difficult (sob)." Most of Hollywood recognizes this plaint for what it is—baloney.

Making Nepotism Work for You If you don't happen to be related to a powerful personage, don't despair. There are two alternatives available:

1. Check your genealogy.
2. Fake it.

Since there are hundreds of celebrities living and working in Hollywood, the chances are excellent that you are, indeed, related to one of them. The relationship may be very distant, but a little kinship is better than none at all. Put together a list of all the famous names you can think of—producers, directors, agents, studio execs, and stars—and ask your grandmother whether she recognizes any of them. If so, exploit it to the hilt.

If not, fake it. Change your last name to Zanuck, Goldwyn, Stark, Mengers, Streep, Lumet, or Coppola. (Stick with the odd names—changing your surname to Redford won't get you anywhere.) Send out some letters using your phony name or names and follow up with a phone call. Don't worry about being found out—most industry people are much too busy to check your genealogies.

The Phony Nepotism Letter

Dear Cousin Zanuck,

Gee, was I surprised when Grandma told me I was related to you! According to her family album, you and I are fourth cousins twice removed on my father's uncle's side. It sure was a coincidence too, since I've been planning to come to Hollywood to try and make it as a star! Grandma (she says she remembers you when you were a little boy) insisted I write first, so that you and I could get together and talk family.

I will call as soon as I arrive!

Love and XXXXX,
Elvira Zanuck

☆ ☆ ☆ ☆ ☆ ☆ ☆ **ALL IN THE FAMILY** ☆ ☆ ☆ ☆ ☆ ☆ ☆

Famous Name	Relative	Relative's Profession
1. Sam Goldwyn	Sam Goldwyn Jr.	Producer
2. Lloyd Bridges	Jeff and Beau Bridges	Actors
3. Frank Capra	Frank Capra Jr.	Producer
4. Jack Haley	Jack Haley Jr.	Producer
5. Vincente Minnelli	Liza Minnelli	Actress
6. Debbie Reynolds & Eddie Fisher	Carrie Fisher	Actress
7. Henry Fonda	Jane & Peter Fonda	Actress/Actor
8. Francis Ford Coppola	Carmine Coppola	Composer
9. Desi Arnaz & Lucille Ball	Lucie Arnaz	Actress
10. Ronald Reagan	Patti Davis	Starlet
11. Ryan O'Neal	Tatum O'Neal	Actress
12. Alan Ladd	Alan Ladd Jr.	Producer
13. Charlton Heston	Fraser Heston	Producer/Writer
14. Kirk Douglas	Michael Douglas	Producer/Actor

☆

Money Talks

In Hollywood money not only talks louder than anywhere else, it won't shut up. It not only opens doors, it unrolls the red carpet. It makes grovelers out of tyrants, supplicants out of superiors, mistresses out of everyone. It can get you the best table in the best restaurant, meetings with the mightiest of the mighty, and even your very own star on Hollywood's Walk of Fame. It has its own momentum.

So what else is new? The fact is, money *can* buy success in Hollywood. More than that, money *is* success in Hollywood. Of course, the more you have the merrier. Oilman Marvin Davis waltzed into town one day and bought Twentieth Century-Fox. Some people snickered (after all, what does an *oilman* know about making movies?), but those who understood where the clout comes from were lining up to polish the new boss's shoes before the check was even cashed. In Hollywood money is clout.

Needless to say, the glitz and glamour of the industry attracts all kinds of money— big money, medium money, and so-so money. (In Hollywood big money is known as Serious Money.) Though the tax-shelter status of filmmaking is no longer as attractive as it used to be, thousands of investors still see it as an intriguing way to drop a wad. For their trouble, they can visit the set, rub elbows with the celebrities, and maybe even make a profit.

Serious Money If you've got Serious Money, you don't have to do anything except come to town. Over the years

Hollywood has developed its own method of smelling out big bucks. Within a week the grapevine will have announced your arrival and everyone from the studio head to the maître d' will be disproportionately ingratiating. You will be wined, dined, and taken to all the best parties. You will be supplied with starlets galore. Your name will pop up in all the worthwhile columns and your picture will appear in George Christy's *The Great Life*. Real-estate agents will chauffeur you around Bel Air, and suddenly, as if by divine right, you will be dubbed "a producer."

Slowly, you will be introduced to certain film projects in need of backing. You will be sent scripts and asked for judgments. Suddenly, your opinion will mean more than anyone else's. You will be *the* authority. You will always be right.

Medium Money Shelling out a couple of million to back one film project is an easy, albeit short-lived, means of attaining success in Hollywood. Those not willing to take the risk have several other options at their disposal that can guarantee a more prolonged exposure to the perks of Hollywood. The best method is to start your own production company. With a minimum investment you can rent office space, hire flunkies, and print up your own stationery. Before you know it, agents will start calling, studio execs will start asking you to lunch, and writers will start pitching stories. No one will care whether you know anything about filmmaking—as long as you've got enough money to buy options, the calling, lunching, and pitching will continue ad infinitum. You can go on like this for years without ever getting close to developing, let alone making, an actual motion picture.

So-so Money If you can't afford to buy a studio, back a film, or set up your own production company, instant success is a bit more elusive. However, the neophyte with a small amount of cash can help himself by simply spending it wisely.

Here are a few of the alternatives:

1. *Option Something* You don't have to be a producer to option a script, treatment, book, or article. Anyone can option anything, just as anyone can call himself a producer. The trick is to find a reasonably priced property (i.e., one that costs no more than, say, $2,000). Once you own an option, you can take meetings and, more importantly, go to parties and say, "I took an option on a property."

2. *Rent a Rolls* For a few hundred dollars a day you can scoot around in your very own Corniche. This alone will imply that you are someone.

3. *Charity* A sizable donation might get you an invitation to a benefit, thereby giving you the opportunity to hobnob with the rich and powerful. They, of course, will assume you are one of them.

4. *Self-promotion* For a few thousand you can take out an ad in *Variety* announcing a bogus film project. If *Variety* says you're a producer, you're a producer.

5. *Drugs* Entering a meeting with a vial of cocaine means immediate peer acceptance.

☆☆☆☆☆ WHAT MONEY CAN BUY ☆☆☆☆☆

Item	Approximate Cost
1. Movie studio	$155,000,000 plus
2. Low-budget film	$3,000,000–5,000,000
3. Production company	$25,000
4. Film option	$2,000–10,000
5. PR man	$1,500/month
6. Variety ad	$1,000 plus
7. Sunset Boulevard billboard	$5,000
8. Benefit donation	$200–1,000
9. Rolls-Royce rental	$250 plus
10. Gram of cocaine	$125

☆ ☆

☆

Contacts

Contacts are the next best thing to nepotism. If your old college roommate happens to be a studio exec, a producer, a director, an agent, or a casting director, and you've maintained some sort of communication over the years, you're one step ahead of the game. You won't achieve instant success through contacts, but you'll certainly have a distinct edge.

The contact, however, has to be fairly direct for it to be worthwhile. In other words, just knowing someone whose cousin's girlfriend's father is an agent is too indirect to be of much significant value. The closer the contact the better.

Those who've been around Hollywood for a while know that building a stable of contacts, and maintaining that stable, is a slow but dependable method of achieving success. Hollywood is in many ways a club, and a very exclusive one at that. One of the best ways of gaining membership (short of having serious money or a famous name) is through the contact pyramid.

In the contact pyramid you start with one contact and nurture it along until it leads to two new contacts and so on until you have developed a sizable and upwardly mobile stable.

While building your contacts, however, it is important to be cognizant of the crucial difference between the concept of a contact and the concept of a friend. Although contacts will come on to you as if they are friends, it is always wise to maintain a discreet distance. Friends are those you trust completely, the ones you feel you can voice your inner frustrations to without getting burned. Friends presumably have no ulterior motives.

This is not so with contacts. Maintaining a workable contact can be a fragile endeavor. Contacts will help you along the path to success only if they feel strongly enough that your success will someday benefit *them*. A contact is worthless unless he or she looks upon *you* as a potential contact. In order to maintain this equilibrium, you must continuously create the impression that you are going places. This is accomplished through hype. Hype will be discussed thoroughly in a subsequent chapter.

How to Start a Contact Relationship Imagine that you have just arrived in Los Angeles, set on becoming a director. After leafing through your college alumni paper you discover that one of your old chums is a story editor at a medium-sized independent production company. He is your only potential contact.

One day you call him up at his office. He comes on very strong. You do likewise. He says he'd like to get together sometime. You pin him down to a time and a place. (In Hollywood everyone always wants to get together "sometime.") Pick an expensive, chic restaurant like Ma Maison or Trumps and imply that it is your treat. Make sure the eatery you choose has valet parking. That way, when you leave, he'll see the brand-new Mercedes 380SL you've rented specifically for this occasion.

Prior to arriving at the restaurant, make a reservation in your name and get the first name of the maitre d'. Have your answering service promise to call the restaurant at half-hour intervals and ask to have you paged.

Arrive at least twenty minutes late, but don't make any excuses other than that you were tied up in meetings. Ask your potential contact what he has been up to career-wise. He will probably drop a few names. Make like you're a close personal friend of everyone whose name he mentions. *Never* admit that you don't know someone in Hollywood.

When the conversation gets around to your status and career, drop a lot of names (first names) and imply that you're living in a small condo while waiting for escrow to finalize on the little shack you've just bought in Malibu. Infer that you've gotten so many film and TV directing offers you can't decide which to take. Ask for his advice. Don't worry about him asking for your credits as it is considered impolite in Hollywood to inquire about them.

Pay the bill and leave a generous tip. When leaving, make sure to give the valet your ticket *first*. Otherwise, your contact won't be around to see your brand-new 380SL. If he had any doubts about your spiel at dinner, the 380SL will quiet them. Before driving off, shake hands warmly and say, "Let's do it again, some-time." Chances are he will call within a week.

Needless to say, this contact is strictly a building block. Story editors have little power themselves but, as ambitious souls in their own right, they usually know plenty of writers, producers, and agents. His contacts will soon become your contacts and so on.

Favors "I owe you a favor," is a common Hollywood phrase, one of the few that actually means something. It is important while building contacts to do as many favors for those contacts as possible. This can involve everything from taking someone to the airport to getting a producer together with a writer. When collecting on a favor, never feel embarrassed about reminding someone that they owe you one. Favors are the currency of Hollywood.

☆

A Typical Contact Pyramid

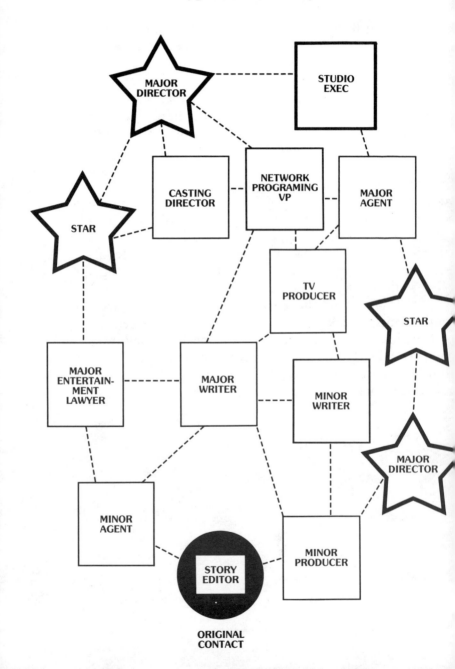

☆

Big in the Apple = Hot in Hollywood

Hollywood has always held a certain begrudging reverence toward the world's cultural centers. Sam Goldwyn, for one, was notorious for importing great talent from Europe and New York. Although he looked up to these men and their work, once they were under contract to him, he did the usual thing: he treated them like flunkies. Yet their mere presence made him feel cultured, worldly, and sophisticated. Most of them didn't stay long.

Hollywood still worships those who have proven themselves in places like New York City. The Big Apple is still considered the center of creative achievement, and it is probably accurate to say that most Hollywood hot-shots feel somewhat insecure when compared to their New York counterparts. In most peoples' minds Hollywood is still in the minor leagues when it comes to culture.

The point of all this is that if you've managed to hit the big time in New York (or Europe), you will almost automatically make it in Hollywood. A major writer in New York is by rights a hot writer in Hollywood. The same goes for Broadway producers, directors, and stars. Many of these people work in Hollywood once in a while to make a fast buck, but few stay.

Though the cachet of New York fame has been big for years in Hollywood, the cachet of foreign fame seems to vary from year to year. In Hollywood, countries are trendy. French and Italian actors and directors were causes célèbres for a while. Swedes had their day some time ago. Britons and Australians have lately been enjoying the limelight. Next year it will probably be some hot new talent from Ulan Bator.

If you're looking for some easy cachet, try a fake British or Australian accent on for size. Invite producers over for high tea. Offer them crumpets and scones instead of coke. Speak at length about your experience directing, acting in, and writing movies in Australia or England. Talk abusively and condescendingly about American cinema. (Hollywood thrives on abuse.) Use phrases like mise-en-scene and auteur and refer to Lord Laurence Olivier as Larry. If nothing else, you'll at least get on a lot of guest lists.

☆ ───────────────────── ☆

High Tea

Some Hollywoodians have become so entranced with the inherent class and status of being British, they've gotten into the habit of taking high tea. Several posh eateries now offer a four o'clock tea menu. Trumps serves scones and cucumber and watercress sandwiches as does the Westwood Marquis. Taking high tea, of course, is an ultra hip thing to do (unless you're English, in which case it is just ordinary).

☆ ───────────────────── ☆

☆☆☆☆ THE WASHINGTON CONNECTION ☆☆☆☆

Since Hollywood and Washington, D.C. are fairly similar when it comes to the nuances of backbiting, patronage, and hype, one simple way of ensuring an instant career in Hollywood is to first pay your dues in the nation's capital by becoming either the President or Secretary of State. Politicians do very well in Hollywood and Hollywoodians do very well in Washington. (Look how easy it was for Ronald Reagan.) In most cases the transition from one place to the other is a painless one. The following three luminaries used Washington as a stepping stone toward a Hollywood career.

Henry Kissinger: on the board of directors—Twentieth Century-Fox
(Globe)

Alexander Haig: on the board of MGM/UA
(Globe)

Gerald Ford: on the board at Fox
(Globe)

☆ ☆

☆☆☆ REPUTATIONS THAT TRAVELED WELL ☆☆☆

Star	Locale of Fame	Hollywood Success
1. Mel Gibson	Australia	Actor
2. David Mamet	New York	Screenwriter
3. Charles Bronson	France	Actor
4. Dino De Laurentiis	Italy	Producer
5. François Veber	France	Screenwriter
6. Liv Ullman	Sweden	Actress
7. Jeremy Irons	England	Actor
8. Werner Herzog	Germany	Director
9. Dudley Moore	England	Actor
10. Louis Malle	France	Director
11. Rutger Hauer	Netherlands	Actor
12. Ridley Scott	England	Director
13. Peter Weir	Australia	Director
14. Rudolf Nureyev	USSR	Actor
15. Jerzy Kosinski	New York	Writer/Actor

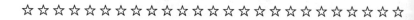

☆ ☆

☆

Hype

Without trying to hype the role of hype in Hollywood, it is fair to state that hype is, without a doubt, the single most important factor in anyone's game plan for success in the industry. It pervades all levels of Hollywood from the lowliest to the loftiest. Many a spectacular career has been built on nothing more substantial than a sturdy foundation of pure, unadulterated hype. More than just a building block in the overall framework of upward mobility, hype has become an accepted way of life in most show-biz circles and should be seriously regarded as an essential tool in the neophyte's rocky climb to the pinnacle! (How's that for hype?)

What exactly is hype? Put in basic terms it is simply the unrestrained use of hyperbole, embellishment, or deception for the purpose of self-promotion. Studios hype their films, agents hype their clients, producers hype their projects. Here, of course, we will be primarily concerned with how you can hype

Hype in action—Ma Maison and the usual assortment of expensive cars deliberately parked in front

yourself, a widespread practice necessary for survival in Hollywood.

In the old days, when actors, writers, directors, and producers were under contract to the studios, hype was relegated to studio publicists and was basically their exclusive terrain. Publicity departments would often do more than embellish—they would invent stage names, fabricate credits, and conjure up phony bios. They would do anything to get attention, which in those days meant getting into the columns. Then (and now) truth in advertising was unheard of. This soon became an acceptable practice, no matter how gross the exaggerations or shameless the fabrications. Nowadays there are still publicists and they still use hype to promote their clients, but at some point in time the clients took up the practice themselves, allowing hype to run rampant.

Hype can be ostentatious or subtle, though it is rarely the latter. In Hollywood you'll see hype manifest itself in party conversations ("I've got a deal pending at Fox"), on the freeway (Rolls-Royces, Mercedes, etc.), in the trades (self-promotional ads and column references), and in the parking lots of restaurants (the fancy cars are deliberately parked in front). Hype is having a deal in the works, driving the right car, being seen at the right restaurants, dropping the right names, having the right agent, knowing the right people. No one in Hollywood is immune from hype.

Since most of us were brought up to be fairly honest about our accomplishments and goals, and to exercise a polite degree of modesty at all times, hype may be difficult to comprehend at first. But once you understand it and realize that its transparency is part of its charm, you'll have no choice but to engage in it wholeheartedly. After all, it is just part of the game. Moreover, hype is contagious. There is no point in being the only one at a party not bragging about a deal.

How to Know When You're Being Hyped Many neophytes who come to Hollywood, unaware of its well-deserved reputation as the world's most prolific hype factory, fall into the trap of believing everything they see and hear. Experienced Hollywood hypers can be very convincing. They usually ooze charm and sincerity, and their favorite prey is the naive newcomer.

Moreover, being hyped can lead to frustration and loss of self-esteem since the trusting neophyte will be led to believe that everyone he meets is wealthy, successful, and content. On the surface it will appear as if absolutely everyone in Hollywood drives a Mercedes, everyone has a deal, and everyone is raking in big bucks. If you are not doing any of these things, you will feel like a dismal failure, particularly in the face of such widespread success. To avoid depression keep the following cardinal rules of hype in mind at all times:

1. Eighty-five percent of everything you hear in Hollywood is pure, unadulterated bull. Deals are not deals until the contracts are signed. Fancy cars can be leased. Anyone can *say* they live in Beverly Hills.

2. Anyone who has really accomplished anything worth bragging about doesn't need to bother.

For a more complete guide to interpreting hype, see the chart, page 47.

Using Hype for Fun and Profit The accoutrements of hype—the Mercedes, the address, the hangouts—will be thoroughly discussed in Part Three, *The Status Game.* Here we will be more concerned with developing a convincing hype spiel, the verbal transmission of hype.

Your hype spiel should, first of all, be delivered with the appropriate degree of ennui. Discussion should be terse—after all, brevity is the soul of hype. Your goal is to impress your victim without sounding like that is your objective. It is also advisable to develop new hype spiels at least once a week—having the same fictitious deal pending at the same studio for over six months is hardly an effective hype.

The following example will illustrate the wrong way and the right way of delivering a hype spiel.

Hype Scenario #1: The Wrong Approach

FADE IN

EXTERIOR—BEVERLY HILLS BACKYARD—NIGHT

We are at a lavish Hollywood pool party, complete with phony luau and Tahitian special effects. Conversation is laid-back and casual. Hawaiian shirts abound. Everyone seems to be drinking Perrier with lime; no one smokes. Through the hubbub, we catch certain phrases out of context: "I'm starting to really get in touch with my feelings." "Fox is very high on the project." "Let's have lunch."

ANGLE—A YOUNG MAN

This is JOE. The first thing we notice about him as he enters the party scene is that he seems out of place. Perhaps he just got off the bus from Omaha. He is smoking a cigarette, drinking a beer, and sporting a three-piece summer suit. He seems nervous and jittery. After finishing his drink, he sidles up to the fake Polynesian bar for a refill.

ANGLE—THE BAR

Sporting a Hawaiian shirt, white pants, white shoes and pukka-shell necklace, MARTY leans casually against the bar and scrutinizes Joe. The following dialogue ensues between them.

> MARTY
> (very casually)
> So, uh, whadaya do?

> JOE
> Me? I'd like to be a screenwriter.
> What do you do?

> MARTY
> (coyly)
> I produce motion pictures.

> JOE
> (excitedly)
> No kidding! Wow! A producer, huh?

> MARTY
> (in monotone)
> It pays the rent.

> JOE
> (still excited)
> What films have you done?

ANGLE—MARTY

He is beginning to lose interest in the conversation. His eyes are wandering toward the other side of the yard.

> JOE
> Say, you know, I'm working on a
> script right now. . . . It's about these
> two guys who . . .

> MARTY
> Uh, excuse me, sweetheart, I think I
> spotted someone I know. Ciao.

Marty walks off leaving Joe to wonder whether he's got bad breath.

FADE OUT

Analysis   This was a scenario fraught with error, all of it on Joe's part. For starters, Joe is clearly a newcomer—the outfit and the drink gave that away immediately, not to mention his unlaid-back disposition and the fact that he was smoking. Why Marty even deigned to talk to him is anyone's guess. The following are Joe's specific mistakes:

Mistake #1: Joe is much too enthusiastic. He shouldn't have blinked when Marty said he was a producer.

Mistake #2: Joe shouldn't have said he'd *like* to be a screenwriter. In Hollywood it is bad form to admit to aspiration. If you'd like to be it, you're it.

Mistake #3: Joe is much too verbal. He is speaking in actual complete sentences. He should stick to catch phrases and buzzwords.

Mistake #4: Joe's biggest mistake was asking for Marty's credits. It is considered bad form to ever attempt to substantiate a hyper's claim. Never ask for someone's credits and they will never ask for yours.

Mistake #5: Joe shouldn't have said he's working on a script; he should have said he's been hired to develop one.

☆

Hype Scenario #1: The Right Approach

FADE IN

SAME HOLLYWOOD POOL PARTY

ANGLE—JOSEPH (formerly Joe)

Wearing designer jeans, Adidas running shoes, a *Hill Street Blues* T-shirt, and a half-day growth of beard, Joseph seems right at home here. Having drained his Perrier with lime, he sidles up to the bar and casually leans on the counter. He is extremely laid-back.

ANGLE—THE BAR

Marty sidles up and scrutinizes Joseph before beginning the dialogue.

MARTY
(casually)
So, uh, whadaya do?

JOSEPH
(more casually)
I write. You?

MARTY
(coyly)
Produce.

JOSEPH
(dryly)
We met at the Paramount wrap
party, right?

MARTY
Could be.

JOSEPH
(coyly)
Just closed a multi-pic-pac at Par.
Hate their offices, don't you?

MARTY
(dryly)
The pits.

JOSEPH
Who you with?

MARTY
CAA. You?

JOSEPH
Morris.

A Typical Hollywood Party

"I'm between agents right now, but CAA is packaging a romantic comedy I pitched last month for Rodney Dangerfield and Meryl Streep. Everyone at the agency is very excited about it."

"Sure, she's unknown *now*, but give me two years and she'll be red hot. Trust me, she's a big talent. Two years, three max."

"Look, we've got a series pilot casting next week. She might be right for the part of the Latino transvestite. Of course, you probably don't want to risk typecasting her. . . ."

"Actually, everyone was really high on your last script, but I ankled for Fox and my boss went indie, so we had to pass on it. Who's your agent?"

Director of Creative Development: Works at major studio but hasn't got a project off the ground yet. Got her job through powerful relatives. Drives a new BMW with sunroof. About to give birth to a future production V.P. Lives in Hollywood Hills.

Screenwriter: Makes his living by selling options but has yet to get screen credit. Has been through six agents in last three years. Great at pitching stories. Drives a leased 380SL. Lives in Los Feliz.

Agent: Has lots of bread-and-butter TV clients but hasn't had a hot one in years. Knows everyone at the Polo Lounge. Goes to Palm Springs every other weekend. Drives a Cadillac Seville. Wants to produce.

Network V.P.: Wants desperately to move up to prime time but seems to be stuck in daytime programming forever. Assuages guilt by subscribing generously to PBS. Drives a Porsche. Lives in Encino.

"Who's he trying to kid? His last epic was unreleasable."

"So I had my facial, my manicure, my pedicure, took a sauna and a Jacuzzi, jogged for an hour, went to aerobics, saw my chiropractor, my therapist, went to yoga class . . ."

"My acting teacher says I overemote. So I've been trying to compensate by underemoting, but my nutritionist says emoting is natural and my acupuncturist doesn't speak English . . ."

"I love the way your mind works. You'd be perfect for my next picture— it's a comedy based on the Tylenol case. How about lunch at Trumps next week?"

"You think you've got problems? Last week my tennis court cracked, my Mercedes mechanic moved back to Germany, and Hank Grant forgot to mention my birthday."

Producer: Started out as an agent, became studio exec, and is now an indie prod. Widely known as a savvy dealmaker. Owns an office building on Sunset Boulevard. Hangs out at Ma Maison. Lives in Bel Air.

Story Editor: Reads and critiques scripts for indie prod. Graduated with honors from UCLA film school. Prides herself on knowing the best gossip. Wants to produce meaningful cinema. Drives a Datsun.

Starlet: Makes good money mostly by appearing in detergent commercials. Once got the lead in a low-budget horror film, which was never released. Friends keep telling her "It'll happen." Drives a red Mustang convertible. Lives in Santa Monica.

Star: Was a bit player until marrying a well-known hyphenate and now stars in all his pictures. Ardently campaigning for role of Mother Teresa in upcoming TV bio-pic. Drives a Clenet.

Director: Started career as a cinematographer of dog food commercials. Got first big break by marrying the star of a TV series. Appeared on a Barbara Walters special after recent drug bust. Drives a Rolls-Royce. Lives in Malibu.

At this juncture Joseph, on the pretext of looking for something in his pants pocket, pulls out his car keys, which are attached to a Mercedes key chain.

JOSEPH
How 'bout lunch sometime? I got a
script in turnaround.

MARTY
Love to.

JOSEPH
(looking afar)
Hey, gotta run. Ciao.

FADE OUT

Analysis Joe, who now uses the name Joseph, has clearly outdone Marty in the hype contest. He looks like he has been around Hollywood even longer than Marty; the *Hill Street* T-shirt signals that he is in with a hip crowd. He fabricated the Paramount wrap party to drive the point home. Moreover, he has led Marty to believe that he is ensconced in an office at Paramount, that he has a deal with them, that he is with a bigger agency than Marty and that he's had a script developed ("I got a script in turnaround"). By asking Marty to lunch he left the desirable impression that he couldn't care less if he ever sees Marty again.

Chances are Marty will take the bait and call *him*.

☆ ☆ ☆ ☆ ☆ ☆ ☆ INTERPRETING HYPE ☆ ☆ ☆ ☆ ☆ ☆ ☆

Hype	Probable Interpretation
1. Mercedes 380SL	The car is rented or leased.
2. Mention in Hank Grant's column	The deal is a figment of the producer's imagination.
3. Beverly Hills address	The hyper bought the place when it was cheap and can't afford to furnish it yet.
4. "I just wrote a *Quincy*."	"I just wrote a *Quincy* episode but no one bought it."
5. "I've got a deal pending at Warner's."	"I've got a script that my agent thinks Warner's might like."
6. "I'm up for a part in Hill Street Blues."	"I auditioned for a walk-on on Hill Street Blues."
7. "I'm a producer."	"I'd like to be a producer but I make my living selling Jacuzzis."
8. "I live off Mulholland Drive."	"I live five miles from Mulholland Drive, in Van Nuys."
9. "I'm a writer but I'd really like to direct."	"I wrote a script, couldn't sell it, and I'm frustrated."

☆ ☆

─────────────────── ☆ ───────────────────

Chutzpah

An aspiring director got his start by somehow finagling his way onto a studio lot and commandeering a vacant office. He misrepresented himself as a producer with an office on the lot and made a lot of calls from there. It wasn't long before he got his first big break.

★

A fledgling writer-director with an idea for a horror film found out where a well-known producer went for saunas. Wrapped in a towel, he got into the steam room and, after some casual conversation, began to pitch his story. The producer loved it and gave him a deal. The film came out to good reviews and a solid box office.

★

A frustrated screenwriter with no credits managed to get onto a studio lot. He drove to the office of a famous producer and, without getting out of his car, tossed the script through the producer's open office window. The producer read the material, liked it, and bought it.

★

An unknown actress heard that an established director was looking for an actress with a British accent. She went to the audition and pretended to be English. She got the role and is now successful.

★

The above are factual examples of how a little chutzpah can pay off big in Hollywood. Naturally, for every example of successful chutzpah, there are probably hundreds of failed attempts. Yet chutzpah is a necessary ingredient in any recipe for Hollywood success. Those devoid of chutzpah have no business even being in Hollywood in the first place.

Always keep one thing in mind: *the worst possible response you can get from a show of chutzpah is a simple, "Get lost!"*

To succeed, however, some creativity must be utilized. Chutzpah must be carefully plotted and planned so as not to leave the aspirant feeling like a total moron. There is nothing more embarrassing than the result of half-hearted chutzpah. Self-confidence must be displayed at all times. Moreover, the act itself should be as amusing as possible—an air of levity is essential. You will be judged by your victim on the basis of originality, creativity, and downright gall.

There is, of course, a fine line separating chutzpah from its extreme counterpart, harassment. Chutzpah is considered admirable; it implies guts, aggressiveness, determination, and confidence—all worthy attributes for anyone trying to make it in Hollywood. Harassment, on the other hand, smacks of amateurishness; it implies a lack of judgment and good taste. Chutzpah can easily become harassment if it is exercised repetitiously on an unreceptive audience.

Always keep one thing in mind: *the worst possible response you can get from a show of harassment is, "You'll never work in this town again."*

Chutzpah or Harassment?

☆ ☆ ☆ ☆ CHUTZPAH VS. HARASSMENT ☆ ☆ ☆ ☆

Chutzpah	Harassment
1. Barging into a producer's office and making a pitch while he is in a meeting.	Barging into a producer's home and making a pitch while he is in bed with his mistress.
2. Leaving your resumé in a casting director's car.	Spray-painting your resumé onto a casting director's car.
3. Breaking into a tap dance at a star-studded premiere.	Breaking into a tap dance at a star-studded funeral.
4. Impersonating a journalist to secure an interview with a producer.	Impersonating an IRS auditor to secure an interview with a producer.
5. Publishing a self-promotional ad in the trades.	Publishing a suicide threat in the trades.
6. Bribing a palmist to mention your name while reading a producer's palm.	Bribing a hit man to mention your name while breaking a producer's palm.

☆ ☆

The Casting Couch

A typical Casting Couch

In bygone days the casting couch was a fairly dependable means of getting ahead in the Hollywood rat race. Nubile young starlets with negligible acting ability could distinguish themselves from the competition by bestowing sexual favors in exchange for advancement, provided they at least had a modicum of talent (for sex, not acting). In those days, since Hollywood was largely controlled by heterosexual males, choosing a "sugar daddy" was no problem—producers, agents, and directors were all considered fair game. Sleeping your way to the top could yield real results, provided it was done with discretion and involved no public scandal.

Times have changed, however, and so has the role of the casting couch. Hollywood is no longer the exclusive realm of heterosexual males—nowadays choosing a quarry without a program can be perilous, not to mention embarrassing. Today the nubile young male actor has as good a chance of succeeding via the casting couch as the nubile young starlet. Moreover, sex is not the rare commodity it used to be; no longer considered a favor, sex in modern-day Hollywood is more of an obligation. Discretion is of little consequence and scandal is clearly a thing of the past.

The casting couch, reupholstered in contemporary fabrics, is still a viable way of climbing the ladder. Starlets who develop romantic affiliations with agents, producers, or directors can still find their rise to stardom meteoric if they're canny and wise enough to know how to jump from one casting couch to another without ruffling anyone's feathers. In Hollywood it is taken for granted that producers will give roles to their mistresses, and some studio execs have been known to proffer lofty positions to their bedmates. And, needless to say, a fledgling screenwriter romantically associated with a powerful enough director or hyphenate (see Glossary for definition) will more than likely leapfrog ahead of the competition. After all, the casting couch is really nothing more than a temporary form of nepotism.

The only real taboo is the one-night stand or "quickie." To get anywhere in Hollywood via the casting couch, you have to be respected in the morning. The idea is to use your liaison to gain entry into the in crowd. In other words be prepared to have a "relationship," either meaningful or otherwise. Although this may seem like more trouble than it is worth, keep in mind that in Hollywood, a meaningful relationship lasts no longer than thirty minutes.

☆

The Hard Way—Talent

Attempting to make it in Hollywood on talent alone is like trying to climb Mount Everest on ice skates: it is courageous in a foolhardy sort of way, but hardly the most efficient means of transportation. It can also take years.

Defining talent is part of the problem. One man's talent is another man's hack. To an agent a talent is a person who requires a minimum effort to sell. To a director a talent is someone who massages his ego and never questions his authority. To a producer a talent is someone who has already been dubbed a talent by everyone else. In Hollywood if you're "hot," you're talented; if you're not, you're not.

Moreover, talent is directly proportional to box-office success. In other words everyone associated with a picture that makes millions is immediately a big talent, especially the director since he is usually most adept at garnering the lion's share of the credit. Critical success is always nice, but commerciality is crucial.

If you're a purist (and something of a masochist as well), it is possible to make it on talent alone. Diehard tenacity and unflagging confidence are necessary attributes for this path. Be advised, however, that Hollywood will do its utmost to subvert your resolve. Those who don't play by the rules are seldom popular.

No matter which method or combination of methods you employ to make it big in Hollywood, it is always advisable to keep abreast of events both socially and businesswise. Hollywood thrives on gossip and innuendo and, needless to say, every rung of the ladder has its very own built-in gossip mill. Without access to those gossip mills your best bet is to get whatever news you can from the various local publications that supply the community with something to gab about. Certain sections of these publications should be read religiously, and information should then be passed on to others at parties and lunches in the appropriately jaded manner.

By and large the Hollywood press has a fairly healthy attitude toward its beat. Journalists who cover the industry have either not succeeded in making it in the industry or, more often, don't give a damn about making it in the industry—if they did they'd be making ten times as much money writing scripts. As a result their reportage is usually acerbic and distinctly lacking in the sort of enthusiasm one might expect.

The following is a comprehensive list of publications offering the best inside info to anyone not privy to the gossip mills:

1. *Variety* The daily version has more news and inside poop. Readers should always peruse Army Archerd's "Just for *Variety*" column and the "Pix, People, Pickups" section. The weekly has the famous "50 Top Grossing Films" chart, the industry's favorite scoreboard of hits and flops.

2. The *Hollywood Reporter* The town's other trade publication, the *Reporter*, is issued daily and provides more social news than *Variety*. Of special interest, more for laughs than news, are Hank Grant's "Off the Cuff" column, which contains information on deals that rarely come to fruition, and George Christy's society column, "The Great Life," which features photos and chitchat from the local party circuit.

3. The *Los Angeles Times Calendar section* provides local reviews and some entertainment gossip. Two sections—"The Video File" and "Film Clips"—should be perused whenever they appear.

5. *Beverly Hills People* Distributed free at banks and reception lounges, *BHP* is strictly a social organ with special emphasis on the social activities of old-line Hollywood.

4. The *Los Angeles Herald Examiner* Humorously written anecdotes about the latest industry gaffes appear on Page 2, Hollywood's only real newsprint gossip column.

6. *Los Angeles Magazine* A monthly glossy, *LA Mag* brims with Rodeo Drive ads and restaurant listings. Its "Insider" column offers interesting industry gossip, usually from high-level inside sources.

How to Read the Trades

Variety and the *Hollywood Reporter,* commonly known as "the trades," are the business news organs of the industry. They are read religiously by everyone in the film biz from the bottom up. If you want your name to reach the desks of the high and the mighty, the quickest way is through the trades.

Reading them correctly, however, requires a bit of basic training since both seem to have created their own language. For example, what exactly does *Variety* mean when it proclaims: "PAR VID FEEVEE SERIES TO SKED," or "WB LONGFORM TV AREA LEADER?"

☆ ─────────────────────────────── ☆

The following glossary should shed some light on the subject:

VarietySpeak	Translation
1. Par, U, WB, Col, 20th	Paramount, Universal, Warner Bros., Columbia, Twentieth Century-Fox
2. Vid	Video
3. Feevee	Pay TV
4. Sked	Schedule
5. Longform	Feature length or longer
6. NATO	*Not* the North Atlantic Treaty Organization—the National Association of Theater Owners
7. Ink	Sign a contract
8. Topline	Star in
9. Biopic	Biographical film
10. BO	*Not* body odor—box office
11. Boffo	Doing very well, as in, "E.T. was boffo at the box office."

12. Ankle	Leave; to walk away; to resign, as in "Sherry Lansing ankled her position at Fox."
13. Legs	Endurance at the box office. If a film continues to do well after the first week, it is said to have legs.
14. MOW	Movie of the week (TV)
15. Gotham	New York City
16. The Hub	Boston
17. Bows or preems	Premieres
18. Helm	Direct
19. Pen	Write
20. Indie prod	Independent producer

How to Get Your Name in the Trades

Basically, there are two ways of getting your name in either *Variety* or the *Hollywood Reporter:*

1. Take out a full-page self-promo ad. This method works particularly well for attractive young women with outstanding measurements seeking careers in film or television.

2. Send them an official press release. When there is space, both of these trades will fill up the gaps with press release information. To send one you can forego the expense of hiring a public relations person. The PR person will just charge you $1,500, type a press release up, and send it to the trades. Type up your own and put it in the mail. You will have a 50 percent chance of seeing it in print.

The Phony Press Release

FLIM-FLAM PUBLIC RELATIONS, INC.

6750 Wilshire Boulevard, Suite 600, Beverly Hills, CA 90068

Telex: HOTAIR

December 7, 19—   IMMEDIATE RELEASE

   Broadway sensation _____(your name)_____ has been signed to _____(write, direct, star in)_____ Cheapshot Productions' film adaptation of *The Dead Sea Scrolls*. Winner of the prestigious _____(regal-sounding name)_____ Award for _____(acting, directing, writing)_____, Mr./Ms. _____(last name)_____'s credits are too numerous to mention. *The Dead Sea Scrolls* will mark his/her _____(acting, directing, writing)_____ debut. Production is scheduled to commence in April of 19—.

Beverly Hills   New York   London   Paris   Cracow

PART TWO

Let's Make a Deal!

☆ ☆

Movers and Shakers

Before getting into our discussion of the engrossing drama of Hollywood deal-making, it might be instructive to introduce the cast of characters usually involved in any typical deal. Although deal-making can peripherally involve any number of people, the main participants are the agent, the producer, and the studio exec. These are Hollywood's Movers and Shakers.

In portraying the Movers and Shakers, generalizations will be made. Naturally, no two agents or producers are exactly alike, but most of them do exhibit certain traits common to the species. We will also provide case studies of the other Hollywood caste—the creative community—which includes screenwriters, directors, and actors.

☆

The Agent

"Good career move."
—Anonymous agent, after hearing the
news that Elvis Presley had died.

The agent is a key player in the complex game of Hollywood deal-making. In effect he is the middleman, the human link (or buffer zone) between the creative community (actors, writers, and directors) and the business element (producers and studio execs). Without agents the creative people would have to negotiate directly

DATE _May 5, 1963_ HOUR _12:42_

TO _Marty Fastbuck_

WHILE YOU WERE OUT

M _Sid Hack_

OF _Client_

PHONE _____

AREA CODE		PHONE NUMBER	
TELEPHONED		RETURNED CALL		LEFT PACKAGE	
PLEASE CALL	X	WAS IN		PLEASE SEE ME	X
WILL CALL AGAIN		URGENT	X	IMPORTANT	X

MESSAGE

Has left 23 messages and wants you to get back to him A.S.A.P.

ML-1477 SIGNED _Kate Buffer_

The Agent's favorite ploy— the unreturned phone call

with the business people, which is hardly a pleasant prospect for either party.

More importantly, the agent is a salesman and, like most good salesmen, his primary interest and motivation is money. This is as it should be, but it puts the agent into the position of having to choose his clients more on the basis of their proven earning power than their talent. Since agents get 10 percent of a client's earnings, they cannot afford to waste a lot of time taking chances on newcomers. Ten percent really isn't very much unless the client is raking in millions or if he is what is commonly known as a "bread-and-butter client," usually one who receives a steady paycheck as a TV staff writer or story editor.

Naturally, not every agent in Hollywood is a high roller. Tinseltown abounds with minor agents and managers who do not operate in the mainstream of Hollywood power. Here, however, we will be more concerned with the big, powerful agents (i.e., those who represent big, powerful clients).

Talent vs. Literary Basically, there are two kinds of agents in Hollywood—literary agents and talent agents. If you are a screenwriter and, over drinks in the Polo Lounge, your agent refers to Talent, don't be flattered because he isn't referring to you. Writers are not officially designated as Talent. Actors are Talent. This is a distinction created by agents and unwittingly illustrates the high regard most of Hollywood has for writers.

Talent agents arrange auditions for actors, book engagements, take meetings with producers on behalf of actors, and negotiate contracts. Since many actors are beset by basic insecurities, agents often act as surrogate parents or amateur psychiatrists, particularly if the actor in question is a "money-maker." It is understood that an agent will bend over backwards to keep a valuable client happy, no matter what that requires.

Literary agents attempt to acquire work for screenwriters, directors and, sometimes, producers, take and arrange meetings for them, negotiate contracts and, as has lately become the norm, attempt to package projects. In Hollywood the term "literary," is not meant to be taken seriously.

The Runaround In keeping with the basic, overall philosophy that governs most Hollywood relationships, the agent is rarely available when a client wants to talk to him. This makes the agent difficult to pin down. It also makes most clients paranoid and crazy. Of course, the agent may very well be available when the client is informed otherwise, but the client is usually given the runaround out of principle. The person who makes this eternal charade possible is the agent's secretary. She is the one who answers the phone and immediately offers the standard excuse that the agent is either "on the other line" or "in a meeting." (Variations include "in conference" or "on long distance.") This not only dispatches the caller for the time being, but creates the desirable impression that the agent is very busy, very important, and very much in demand. The Runaround is a form of hype.

Conversely, agents are also notoriously bad about returning telephone calls. The speed with which a call is returned is directly proportional to the client's earning power. A hot client can expect to hear back within an hour or so; a lukewarm client can expect to hear back when he or she qualifies for medicare. This practice serves to explain why most people in Hollywood change agents about as often as they change linen.

Entertainment Lawyers Real status is having a high-powered agent *and* an entertainment lawyer. (Some just have ELs). Generally speaking, entertainment lawyers are better at negotiating and writing iron-clad contracts, especially for those with a lot to gain or lose. Most Hollywood ELs work on contingency, but some demand high retainers, so if you're not raking in the big bucks, don't bother retaining one.

☆

Choosing an Agent

Getting the right agent may be the most important initial step you take in climbing the Hollywood ladder. Without a good, reputable agent you are, for all intents and purposes, a nonentity. A name agent means more status at social gatherings and more clout at meetings. After all, when hustling yourself it is absolutely essential to be able to say, "My people will be in touch with your people," and have some well-known people to back you up.

In many circles your potential will be judged by what agency represents you.

There are hundreds of agents in Hollywood, but only a handful are powerful enough to guarantee clout by association. Having the right agent can be a key status symbol.

In terms of tangible results, however, you must ask yourself this important question: do you want a big agent with lots of clout or do you want a minor agent with lots of patience? In Hollywood the two traits are mutually exclusive.

Most newcomers would opt for the former (clout) without giving the matter much thought, but the fact is, being represented by a big agent has definite drawbacks. For starters a big agent has lots of big clients. Since, presumably, you will not start your career as a big client, you will be at the bottom of his list of priorities. This means you will see him maybe once a year for a drink at the Polo Lounge and most of your calls will go unreturned for up to a decade. You will have lots of clout by association but little attention.

The advantage of having a big agent is simply that he can get the attention of powerful producers and stu-

---

Hollywood Lore

A certain TV actor, tired of being known solely as a TV actor, approached his William Morris agent with the idea of appearing in a play. At first the agent tried to talk him out of it, but sensing his client's determination, he finally gave in.

"What kind of play were you thinking of doing?" the agent asked.

"I was thinking of doing Anouilh," said the client.

The agent shrugged. "A newie, an oldie, what's the difference?"

dio execs. If he should by some miracle recall your name when he is in the presence of the powerful, your career can take off. But the odds of this happening are painfully slim.

On the other hand, the advantage of having a minor agent is that he will most likely lavish attention upon you, at least while he tries to sell you or until he loses interest. (Most agents are not especially tenacious—a fast buck is still a fast buck.) He, too, will take you to the Polo Lounge, probably with more frequency, though *you* might be asked to pick up the tab. For the first two months he may actually even return your phone calls before an indecent amount of time has elapsed.

The disadvantage, of course, is that he will have very little clout and deal primarily with lower echelons of the Hollywood hierarchy, although he will make you believe that he has an inside track to the upper echelons. Worse yet, you will possess the exact opposite of clout by association—anonymity by association.

What to Look for in an Agent Most agents aren't going to win any personality contests. Hollywood is a rough town and they're caught right in the crossfire. They may ooze charm from every pore and speak in glowing, optimistic terms about your future, but this is just business as usual. Don't fall for the pie-in-the-sky routine. An agent who is unsure about your potential is worth more than an agent who promises you the moon.

Understanding Agentese

Hollywood agents rarely say what they mean or mean what they say. Since their primary responsibility is to keep their clients happy in an atmosphere of constant rejection, most agents have been known to resort to certain catch phrases, which (at least on the surface) sound flagrantly optimistic. The following will help the neophyte interpret exactly where his agent is coming from:

When an agent says . . .	He really means . . .
1. "I read your script."	"My secretary read your script."
2. "I'll get back to you tomorrow."	"I'll get back to you next March."
3. "I would have returned your call sooner but I've been tied up in meetings."	"I would have returned your call sooner but there's been no action on your material."
4. "Paramount is very high on the project."	"Paramount is the only studio that hasn't rejected the project."
5. "We've decided to package your material."	"It's still on the shelf."
6. "Marty says you're perfect for the part."	"Marty owes me a favor and will let you audition for the part."
7. "Sid *loved* the script."	"Sid's story editor loved the script."
8. "We're waiting for the best bid."	"We're waiting."
9. "Let's have lunch."	"Have a nice life."

The Top Five Agencies

1. *The William Morris Agency* Still numero uno, the Morris Agency handles everyone—talent and literary. Big on packaging.

2. *International Creative Management (ICM)* Running a close second to William Morris, this agency has offices all over the world. Talent and literary.

3. *Creative Artists Agency (CAA)* Relatively new but extremely powerful, CAA has been taking clients away from the top two for years.

4. *Agency for the Performing Arts (APA)* An excellent agency for talent, especially comedians. Their literary department is relatively new.

5. *Adams, Ray & Rosenberg* Mainly literary, but they also represent directors and producers.

☆

The Producer

"Let's bring it up to date with some snappy nineteenth-century dialogue."
—Sam Goldwyn

The producer is the person who theoretically puts together all the elements required to make a motion picture. Generally, he is the one who either originates the concept or options the original property (book, script, or treatment), supervises the screenwriter's initial drafts, hires the director and the name talent, deals with getting the picture financed, and sees to its distribution. He is the one who nurtures the project along from the first seed of concept to the harvest of celluloid. If it bombs, he is commonly held responsible; if it is boffo, the credit invariably goes to the director.

Though fairly prestigious in the Hollywood hierarchy, producing is not always the most glamourous of jobs. The producer functions largely as the behind-the-scenes manipulator during the deal-making process and,

occasionally, as the invisible glue that holds the principles together during the production stage. He is the guy who has to talk the leading lady back after she has walked off the set, has to reprimand the director for violating the budget, and has to keep the cinematographer sober during production. He is, in other words, the boss, and partly for this reason he is not always universally liked by those with whom he works. Screenwriters often dislike him because he tends to inflict his "creative input," upon their scripts. Directors frequently resent him because he invariably fails to see the artistry involved in violating the budget. Agents are wary of him because he likes to keep them dangling. Studio execs distrust him because without him they wouldn't know how to make films. What motivates people to take on such a thankless task? Simple—money and power.

Producers usually make out better with money than anyone else. Studios pay them hefty fees to develop motion picture projects and, if the project makes it to production, the producer usually ends up with most of the points. In terms of clout, just *being* a producer in Hollywood is like having the recipe for an aphrodisiac.

Like the agent, the producer spends most of his time taking meetings and doing lunches. He often picks up the tab, unless he is a "bogus producer" (i.e., one who just *says* he's a producer but hasn't come close to producing anything yet). Most producers are even more adept than agents at giving people the runaround, since the producer's secretary has, at her command, more than the usual number of standard put-offs (i.e., "He's in Cannes for the month," or "He's on location till March," etc.).

Creative Input There is an old Hollywood saying: "Those who can, do. Those who can't, produce." Many producers are producers simply because they don't have what it takes to be writers or directors. As a result most producers feel that they know more about writing than writers and more about directing than directors. Consequently, they feel compelled to inflict their "creative input," on a film project in almost every stage of its development.

Sam Goldwyn's line about bringing a film up to date with some snappy nineteenth-century dialogue is a good example of creative input. Occasionally, a producer's input can help a faltering project, but often it is counterproductive. Over the years writers and directors have developed a deaf ear for creative input.

Line Producers Most producers don't know the first thing about the actual mechanics of filmmaking. Their job is simply to buy options, take meetings, package material, do lunch, take meetings, handle finance, and take meetings. For this effort they usually get a producing credit and lots of money if the movie is actually shot. These producers often hire what is known as a "line producer" (or "hands-on producer") to see to the actual administration of the film in pre-production, post-production and during the actual filming. The line producer is responsible for dealing with budgetary matters, hiring the crew, and making sure everything is going all right while the other producer stays home and takes meetings, does lunch, and initiates new projects. In some cases the initial producer is also a line producer.

Budgets Film budgets basically divide into two areas: *above-the-line costs* and *below-the-line costs*. Above-the-line costs include fees paid to the major stars, director, screenwriter, and producer—the big salaries. Above-the-line costs are often difficult to pare down. Below-the-line costs incude everything else—technical costs, location costs, crew, drugs, costumes, special effects, drugs, extras, and drugs. Below-the-line costs are usually lower than above-the-line costs.

Interpreting Producerese

Producers have their own peculiar way of expressing themselves. Like agents, they don't like to be pinned down to a definite yes or no on anything. They like to keep their options open and hedge their bets. For example, in producerese, the word "high," connotes a positive attitude just short of a definite yes, such as, "We're very high on the project." This doesn't mean the producer is going to actually consummate a deal, but it does manage to paint a somewhat optimistic picture and gives the agent something nice to convey to his client. If the producer ultimately decides to forego the project, the fact that he was "high," on it becomes entirely meaningless.

Conversely, a producer will never actually say *no* to a project. Producerese for no, is to *pass* on a property. For example, "We've decided to *pass* on the project." This basically means no, but it implies that the rejection is only temporary, and that the producer might one day become "high," on the project if external events suddenly make it more attractive.

Producers like to describe new film projects in terms of existing films. This gets the point across without the use of adjectives and implies that the project in question is worth more than it really is. To illustrate, if a producer is touting a script about a bunch of wild and crazy teenagers who wreak havoc on motorcycles, he is liable to refer to the project as "*Animal House* on wheels." Aside from painting a clear picture of the film's premise, the producer has also managed to sneak in a little sales pitch, since *Animal House* fared rather well at the box office. Sometimes, however, this practice can get a bit out of hand when a producer says, "It's a combination *Kramer vs. Kramer* and *Tootsie*, with a little *Friday the 13th* thrown in for good measure."

☆

The Making of a Producer

How do people become producers? The following are a few of the standard paths.

1. The easiest way to become a producer is to simply go around saying you're a producer. Chances are no one will ask to see any proof. Producers don't need licenses, college degrees, or, for that matter, any experience in filmmaking. If the idea of being a producer appeals to you, you're in business.

2. If you've got money, you can buy an option on a property. This automatically makes you a producer and allows you to work with writers, directors, and agents to develop the property. If you've got a lot of money to throw away, you can even start your own production company and hire people who know what they're doing.

3. Some people in Hollywood dislike producers so much that they *become* producers. These people are generally writers or directors who want to have full control over their own projects and not be compelled to deal with other people's creative input. Writers, actors, and directors who become producers are commonly known as "hyphenates," because their credit lines are full of hyphens, such as "writer-producer-director." The only real disadvantage to being a hyphenate is that if the film bombs you get *all* the blame.

4. Big agents with big clients sometimes become producers because they're fed up with being agents, are tired of taking abuse from producers, and/or would like to make more money. Big agents who package material know the ropes well enough to make an easy transition to the role of producer.

5. A studio exec might decide to become a producer because he feels the need to have more direct control over a film project, wants to make more money or, more often, because his boss has strongly suggested it. Generally, a studio exec who is let go ends up with a fairly lucrative production deal as a form of severance pay from his former studio.

6. A star might decide to become a producer in order to exert full creative control over a project, because it looks like fun, or because he'd like to make more money. Once a star becomes a producer, however, it becomes self-defeating to storm off the set or throw tantrums. For most stars this takes all the fun out of filmmaking.

The Studio Exec

"The trouble with this business is the dearth of bad pictures."

—*Sam Goldwyn*

As the title implies the studio exec is an executive under the gainful employ of one of the major studios. He or she can have any number of official titles, each of which comes with a particular set of functions. A vice-president in charge of production, for example, oversees the production of a film which the studio is backing. A director of creative development supervises the development of a property which the studio owns. There are studio execs for every aspect of a film's evolution including distribution, advertising, publicity, marketing and merchandising, to name a few.

Like their counterparts in other areas of the general business community, studio execs jockey for position, undercut rivals, brown-nose the boss, pass the buck, dress for success, and make decisions based largely on furthering their careers. The difference in the case of studio execs is that the product that generally suffers from all this executive self-preservation is a motion picture.

When a studio decides to give the "green light" to a film project, it usually involves astronomical sums of money. Aside from the prohibitively high production costs (a low-budget studio feature is now in the $7 million range), distribution and advertising are also costly. (Many ad budgets equal the production costs of the film.) For a typical low-to-medium-budget flick a studio could end up shelling out from $12 million to $15 million. If the film is a whopping success, the studio stands to make the lion's share of the profit (points are generally not given out until the studio has recapped its investment). On the other hand, if the film is a bomb, the studio can lose its shirt. It follows that when the studio makes a tidy profit on a film, hordes of studio execs scramble to take the credit for bringing in the project. Conversely, when a film bombs, it is practically impossible to find a studio exec who has even *heard* of the project.

The Risk Factor Since so much money is involved in filmmaking, most studio execs shy away from any project that seems risky. As a result they tend to green light only those projects that come to them already packaged with big stars, name directors and writers and/or producers with proven track records. In other words, given the choice between backing a film project involving an unknown writer, director, and unknown actors, and a project written by Neil Simon, directed by Herb Ross, and starring Jack Lemmon and Walter Matthau, the studio exec will invariably opt for the latter. Neil Simon's films always do quite well at the box office; they are relatively inexpensive to make; and the talent involved usually works within budget and schedule. There are few—if any—variables. Even if the unknown project is far superior, the studio exec will probably pass on it unless either his position in the hierarchy is secure or he can get enough of his associates to back him up. This serves to explain why Hollywood tends to keep putting out the same dreary formula pictures year after year.

The Revolving-Door Syndrome One of the more disconcerting aspects regarding studio execs, at least in the eyes of the creative community, is their tendency to move from one studio to another with annoying regularity. The reason is basic: like all business executives, studio execs desperately want to keep moving up the ladder. Moving from one studio to another at least gives the impression that some sort of upward momentum is under way, even if the change is merely a lateral one. (The average shelf life of a studio exec is about eighteen months.) This process rankles producers, directors, and writers because it tends to spell disaster or at least significant delay for their film projects, which are generally lost in the executive shuffle.

The Story Editor

Story editor is a title with two different meanings. In television the story editor is the person who oversees the development of the script and actively participates in the production of the show. It is a fairly prestigious job and it pays extraordinarily well.

In film the story editor (also known as "reader" or "story analyst") is generally an underpaid, overworked person hired by a studio or independent producer to read all the scripts and treatments submitted, then follow up with a brief critical synopsis for the boss to skim over the weekend. (The weekend is when most of the Biggies catch up on their reading.) It is a thankless position at best since most producers tend to disregard their story editors' critiques, but it is a solid foot in the door to anyone aspiring to bigger and better things. Most story editors hope to matriculate to associate producer or director of creative development and continue upward from there. The stereotypical story editor is a recent graduate of a film school (or the producer's niece) whose goal is to one day become the new Sherry Lansing and make great and meaningful films. Most of them are disabused of this idealistic objective after six months of observing their bosses in action.

☆☆☆☆☆☆☆☆☆☆☆☆☆☆☆☆☆☆☆☆☆

The Creative Community

The creative community generally includes directors, actors, and screenwriters, those whose primary concern is the *art* involved in filmmaking (cinematographers and editors are also in this group). As has often been the case, the creative people, though beneficiaries of most of the glamour attributed to Hollywood, are regarded as little more than pawns by the Movers and Shakers and are usually treated accordingly. That does not imply in the least that the creative people are not necessary—even the Movers and Shakers have to admit, albeit begrudgingly, that without scripts there would be no deals, without directors anarchy would reign on the set, and without actors, there would be no one to speak the lines. Conversely, most members of the creative community will readily admit, albeit begrudgingly, that without agents there would be no one to negotiate contracts, without studio execs there would be no one to distribute movies, and without producers there would be no one to screw up the project.

In other words the creative community and the Movers and Shakers live and work together in a perfectly harmonious symbiotic relationship, fueled by a healthy degree of fear, suspicion, and mutual disdain.

The Director

"That's the trouble with directors—always biting the hand that lays the golden egg."

—Sam Goldwyn

Almost everyone in Hollywood yearns to one day become a director. The familiar phrase, "I'm a (choose one) writer, producer, plumber . . . but I'd really like to direct," still crops up occasionally on the party circuit, cliché-ridden as it has become. Since the director is held to be the author (or *auteur*) of a motion picture, since he has the power on the set, and since he usually ends up with the lion's share of the credit (to the eternal chagrin of the screenwriter), it is little wonder that so many aspire to the profession.

"I'm a plumber but I'd really like to direct."

The director's job usually begins in pre-pro (pre-production). At this stage, along with the producer, his function is to oversee casting, scout locations, help in choosing a crew, and steal the writing credit. Most directors seize this opportunity to assert their own creative vision on the project, provided the producer is amenable. If not, "creative differences" can erupt, a situation that usually leaves the director on the street.

Most directors involve themselves heavily with rewriting the script. In cases where the director is only a quasi-megalomaniac, he will merely make suggestions and let the screenwriter carry the ball. In most cases, however, the director will adhere strictly to the dictates of the *auteur* theory and unashamedly attempt to swipe the screenwriting credit outright. This is generally accomplished by adding enough changes in the original material to cause the Writers Guild Arbitration Committee to permit the director either a share in the credit with the screenwriter or to usurp it completely. Needless to say, this practice does not cause great rejoicing among screenwriters.

On the set the director is, at least theoretically, the boss. That means it is his responsibility to violate schedules and budgets, bawl out the crew for his mistakes, coddle the talent into sublimating their egos for his, and initiate conflicts with the producer over who is in charge. If he has been given "creative control," he can force the producer to keep his creative input to himself for the duration of the shooting schedule. If he has been given "final cut," the studio must refrain from tampering with the last edit of the film. Needless to say, it is the rare director who gets either.

Budgets Some directors appreciate the monetary risks involved in filmmaking and thus do their best to keep well within budgets and schedules. Others, however, consider budgets and schedules as nothing more than plots set up by accountants to hamper their creative flow. These directors generally violate budgets as a matter of principle, insisting that each shot be a carefully crafted work of art even if it requires destroying 200 automobiles and moving the entire cast and crew to the Amazon for better lighting. The most notable recent example of budgetary excess occurred with the film *Heaven's Gate*. Since then the leashes have been tightened on all but the most conscientious directors.

How to Become a Director
People generally become directors in a number of different ways. One method is to first become a producer and hire yourself to direct your next film. This is one of the best ways because, not only do you not need experience, you can give yourself a hefty raise at any time without having to consult anyone. Moreover, if your producer gives you a hard time on the set, all you have to do is tell yourself to shut up. The producer-director position effectively eliminates the possibility of creative differences.

Another common way to break into directing is to become a hot screenwriter and hold out to direct your next script. This eliminates the possibility of the director usurping the screenwriting credit. Screenwriters often make good directors because they possess the original vision of the film. From there it is a short leap to a triple hyphenate (writer-producer-director).

If you don't feel like going to all the trouble of becoming a producer or screenwriter in order to become a director, one of the easier methods is to simply marry a big star. The idea is to cajole your stellar spouse into refusing all projects unless you are put on as director. This usually works because most producers perceive that the star is infinitely more important than the director.

☆ ☆ ☆ ☆ ☆ ☆ ☆ **DIRECTOR TALK** ☆ ☆ ☆ ☆ ☆ ☆ ☆ ☆

Chemistry When the actors in a film develop a harmonious relationship resulting in above-par performances. In other words when the director is able, through cajolery, threats, and/or sheer tyranny, to make his actors sublimate their egos for the sake of the project.

Cinematographer The cameraman, which is a difficult position to achieve unless your father is already in the union. In some cases when the director is a first-timer, the cinematographer will give him informal directing lessons on the set, but graciously allow the director to claim full credit.

Creative control What every director dreams of—immunity from others' creative input.

Cut What the director is supposed to say after a shot has been photographed.

DGA The Directors Guild of America, a difficult union from which to get a membership.

Final cut Even more of a divine privilege than creative control—the right to have the last edit on a film.

Take A run-through of a scene, as in, "Take one," or (if things are going badly) "Take 198."

Wrap The close of shooting, as in, "That's a wrap."

☆ ☆

The Actor

The Hollywood rat race is particularly grotesque for actors. Competition is fierce (it is not unusual for 200 actors to show up for a part in a dog food commercial), good roles are few and far between, and it is the rare producer who is willing to risk millions on a new face. Yet once an actor becomes a star, he can become an unstoppable money machine.

Because Hollywood is so overstocked with would-be actors and actresses, the thespian's ladder to the top has more than the usual number of slippery rungs. For starters the unemployment rate for actors at any given time is approximately 85 percent. Most actors in Hollywood are compelled to spend much of their time doing things other than acting. Many work part time as waiters, waitresses, used-car salesmen (actors make *great* used-car salesmen), or receptionists, take acting classes at night, and go to auditions whenever they can. For actors, just getting into a good acting class or landing an agent who will arrange auditions is a feat in itself. No agent will even sign an actor unless he or she has the right look.

The Right Look The right look varies from year to year. In the forties and fifties Hollywood was primarily interested in hero/heroine types—actors and actresses who were good-looking in a slick, convincing way. In the sixties the anti-hero look was in, brought on by such films as *The Graduate*. In the seventies actresses had to be well-endowed to get roles in TV. Nowadays we're gradually getting back to the hero/heroine look. Those without the prevailing look can still secure secondary roles, but the real money tends to go to those who fit the fad.

Auditions All unknowns are required to submit to Hollywood's various means of organized humiliation. For the budding screenwriter it is the pitch session. For the aspiring actor it is the audition.

Auditions are held for two basic reasons: to fill small roles in a movie or TV show and to help lonely producers and directors meet girls. If you are not a star, and if you are not romantically affiliated with a powerful personage, you'll be compelled to start out with bit roles and hope you'll get noticed. To get bit roles you'll have to audition for them.

In most auditions actual acting ability takes a backseat. (In TV it can even be a drawback.) More important is the right look or attitude. Attitude can be faked, but without the right look there is little you can do, short of overnight plastic surgery, to improve your chances.

Overnight Success In spite of the staggering odds, some actors do manage to make the leap from unknown to star in short order. The best way to arrange meteoric notoriety is to marry someone with enough money to fund a motion picture in which you can star. Having powerful relatives doesn't hurt, either. In both cases be prepared for some flack from the press and the critics when your vehicle is released, but once that subsides (and it will) you'll be in the public eye sufficiently to get on a Barbara Walters Special where you can posture sincerely about how difficult it has been for you to prove yourself.

Occasionally, a producer or director will hold a nationwide talent hunt to find the perfect unknown to fill a big role in a motion picture. This, needless to say, is another method for achieving overnight success though often, the talent hunt is actually nothing more than a publicity gimmick designed to promote the project.

The Screenwriter

Practically everyone living in and around Hollywood has written a script or treatment at some point in his life. The temptation is too great for most to resist. As a result nearly everyone from the waiter at the local Fatburger to the mechanic at the neighborhood filling station lays claim to the title of "writer," or as it is known in more jaded Hollywood circles, "writor." Wri-

ters are a dime a dozen in Hollywood.

The problem is, writing looks easy. Almost anyone who is semiliterate thinks he can do better than the high-priced scribes who actually make a living at it. What most neophyte screenwriters generally fail to grasp is that the actual writing is the easy part. Selling the idea and getting it into development is what separates the men from the boys. This requires knowing how to develop a marketable concept and learning how to pitch it effectively. The actual writing is incidental. (See the following sections on "How to Pitch a Story" and "How to Write a Marketable Screenplay.")

Catch-22s As with every other field of endeavor, screenwriting has its own built-in Catch-22s, developed by Hollywood to discourage anyone who thinks screenwriting is a simple means of getting a foot in the door. Writers lacking credits or previous experience are low on the list for writing assignments. (A lousy credit is worth infinitely more than no credit at all.) Uncredited TV writers are practically banned from the video market. (The networks keep active lists of approved writers with TV credits.) As a result, even if you've managed to sell a series idea, chances are slim you'll be invited to pen the pilot.

The best way to overcome these rigid obstacles is to team up with a credited writer and ride in on his or her coattails. It goes without saying that convincing a credited writer of your worth as a collaborator is much easier than convincing a producer to give you a shot at writing his new series.

The Writer's Goals The primary objective of any writer in Hollywood is the all-important screen credit. This means that your name has actually appeared on a screen and that you are totally to blame for the scripting of the show. Once the screen credit has been established, the writer is well on his way to the big time. He will be offered writing assignments, rewrite jobs, development deals, and the chances of his projects going to principle photography will be slightly better. (Producers have an easier time getting projects off the ground if name writers are attached.) And the more credits you have, the less actual writing you have to do to earn a living.

Naturally, getting an actual screen credit is no simple task. Since the studios develop hundreds of projects each year but only actually make seventy to eighty, the odds are hardly in the writer's favor. But don't despair. Hundreds of screenwriters (in fact, the majority) make perfectly decent livings just selling and renewing options on their material without ever seeing their scripts materialize into celluloid. Many manage to exist quite comfortably on lucrative development deals and rewrite assignments, the results of which end up forever collecting dust in some studio exec's file cabinet. In theory this practice bears a slight similarity to the government's farm subsidy program in which farmers are paid good wages to refrain from growing crops.

The Abuse Factor Since the script is recognized as the most important element in filmmaking, it stands to reason that the screenwriter is Hollywood's prime target for abuse. This is traditional. It is incumbent upon producers to tamper with the screenwriter's work, for the director to swipe his credit, and for the actor to alter his dialogue. He is generally regarded as hired help, easily replaceable by others, not unlike butlers, maids, and handymen. Most professional writers learn to take this in stride since it comes with the territory, preferring to release their angst by seeing therapists, engaging in hostility-reducing exercise programs, or comparing horror stories with other sympathetic writers. Revenge is usually an unlikely possibility since, no matter how successful a screenwriter becomes, the abuse factor usually remains consistent. Only a handful of very successful screenwriters possess the luxury of calling their own shots.

☆

How to Pitch a Story

For the screenwriter, knowing how to effectively pitch a story is vastly more important than knowing how to write one. Once a story is committed to paper in the form of a treatment or script, there is little room for change or embellishment, whereas during the pitch session, the canny inventor can change angles, introduce characters, and alter plots at will. Moreover, the pitch session affords the writer the opportunity to use props, histrionics, and ambiguity to his advantage.

Generally speaking, a writer pitches a story to a producer. This is the norm, though it can vary because stories can be pitched to anyone who will listen—stars, directors, studio execs, even story editors. Pitching to a producer has built-in advantages and disadvantages as listed below:

Advantages The producer is desperate for anything that sounds like a new twist on an old theme. Since he usually doesn't know what he likes, he can easily be persuaded if one knows how to make a mundane plot sound original.

Disadvantages The producer is usually a jaded sort who thinks he has already heard everything at least twice. He will show no signs of life during the pitch session and possibly even go out of his way to answer phone calls during the pitch.

Pitching Strategy To effectively pitch a story a writer has to be more than just a writer—he must be an actor, a casting director, and a director to boot. If the story is a comedy, he must have some knack for stand-up delivery. Remember that the producer who appears to be only half-listening to your spiel wants, more than anything, to be entertained. And, of course, he wants to be persuaded that your idea is the hot one he has been waiting for. Think of him as a piece of clay with a short attention span.

Here are a few basic pointers:

1. Always dress appropriately for the type of story you are pitching. Bright, garish colors are good for comedies—a helicopter beanie is a nice touch. Basic black is fine for horror films. Word has it that *The Exorcist* was sold because the writer was clever enough to bring a thermos of green pea soup to his pitch session.

2. Never make literary references. If a producer perceives that you have anything remotely resembling intellect, he will be wary. Never refer to a plot as being Runyonesque or Hemingwayan—this will not impress the average producer. Always describe overall ideas in producerese, such as, "it's a combination *Citizen Kane* and *Some Like It Hot*."

3. Don't explain your story too much; act it out. Use script language and gestures. For example, "We fade in on the United States Senate. The gavel raps to indicate the chamber is in session. [Rap, rap, rap.] Hubbub ceases. Suddenly, off-camera, we hear the *splat!* of a cream pie that's been thrown in someone's face. Another *splat!* And then another. To find the culprit the camera pans the chamber, finally focussing on a cream pie in midair and following it in close-up until it lands in the already-splattered face of . . . [pause for effect] . . . the President Pro Tempore of the Senate . . . [pause for effect] . . . Chevy Chase."

4. Always suggest casting choices for your material. This will help the producer visualize your characters. But don't overdo it. Laurence Olivier, Bill Murray, Warren Beatty, Barbra Streisand, and Cheech and Chong is a nice casting combination but hardly realistic.

5. Even though you may have already pitched the same tired story ten times before, always feign enthusiasm. No producer is going to get excited by a pitch delivered in monotone.

6. Let the producer arrive at his own conclusions regarding the marketability of your idea. Never say, "This story really panders to the youth market." This fact will presumably be foremost on the producer's mind and

does not require verbalization.

7. Do not be ruffled if the producer answers the phone while you're in mid-pitch, or if he seems to be nodding off, yawning widely, or clearing his throat impatiently. These ruses are all part of the producer's bag of tricks, and he will use them to assert his superiority over you. *Be* ruffled if he leaves the room and doesn't return.

How to Write a Marketable Screenplay

First of all, forget everything you learned in film school. That fascinating course you took in French cinema of the 1930s won't do you a bit of good in Hollywood. Hollywood producers aren't interested in characterization or social value—they're interested in how many teenagers will shell out five bucks a head to go and see your movie. If you know a twelve-year-old, ask him what movies he likes and proceed from there.

The following are a few random pointers:

1. Choose a short title. One-word titles are best since most producers feel that the American movie-going public is too dumb to remember more than one or two words.

2. Forget Westerns. No one in Hollywood is interested in Westerns anymore. Comedies are good provided they are predictable and infantile enough to draw the youth market. Horror films are always in demand. Movies for TV should focus on trendy subjects such as child abuse and wife-beating.

3. Stick to stereotypical characters, particularly when writing for television. Women should be characterized either as bimbos or housewives. Feminist types should be overly stern and humorless. Men should be macho. Blacks and Hispanics are secondary charac-

ters and should always speak in ghetto slang. Old people are crotchety and senile.

4. Always include a romance, even if it is totally gratuitous.

5. Keep dialogue to a minimum and always keep the action going. Hollywood perceives that most of the American public has a low attention span—too low to sit through more than five or six lines of dialogue between car chases.

6. TV series or sitcom treatments should not exceed a page and a half. TV execs feel that the premise of a TV show should be as brief and superficial as possible.

Always Judge a Script by Its Cover

Infinitely more important than the actual substance of a script is the binder that encloses it. Bland, pre-fab binders will simply not do anymore. A screenwriter who wants his material taken seriously will have to spring for a shiny, coated binder with the script's title embossed or debossed professionally into the fabric. Choose your color wisely. Black binders are out—too grim. Bright red will get attention, but maroon or crimson are preferable. Bright yellow and green are considered too flashy.

The Hollywood Casualty List—Writers

The roster of famous scribes whose experiences in Hollywood left something to be desired is a long and impressive one. Nathanael West was hired to adapt *Miss Lonelyhearts* for the screen, but no one took his input seriously. Ernest Hemingway was almost thrown out of L. B. Mayer's office by security guards. F. Scott Fitzgerald's experience was one of total frustration. James Jones and John O'Hara weren't overly fond of the place, either. William Faulkner, who got a screen credit for *The Big Sleep*, had the right idea—he came when he needed some fast money and promptly left.

Hollywood Casualty List—Writers

Fitzgerald *(Wide World)*

Faulkner *(Wide World)*

Hemingway *(Wide World)*

Jones *(Globe)*

☆ ☆

Deal-Making

"A verbal contract isn't worth the paper it's written on."
—Sam Goldwyn

It is a popular misconception that people in the movie industry spend most of their time making films. If this were true, Hollywood would churn out more than twice as many films per year as it currently does, since the actual production time of the average film is no more than six months (two months for shooting and four months for arguing over credits). The fact is, industry people spend most of their time talking on the phone, taking meetings, and doing lunches. (In Hollywood meetings are *taken* and lunches are *done*.) What do they hope to accomplish through all this talking, taking, and doing? They hope to make what is commonly known as "the deal."

The deal is the single most important aspect of film-making. This is because it has to do with money. Without the deal there would be no Rolls-Royces, no heated swimming pools, no trips to Cannes, no shopping sprees on Rodeo Drive. There would also be no movies. For it is only after the deal has been made that the mythical money machine switches on and the ball starts rolling toward the ultimate goal of making a motion picture. Never mind that most deals fall through—enough people make enough money along the way to make deal-making a profitable end in itself. If nothing else, it keeps a lot of nice restaurants in business. The deal-making process is worth examining because it is one of the primary reasons Hollywood churns out so many ill-con-

The ever-popular Polo Lounge (or more commonly, Polio Lounge), where many high-level Deals are still made *(Courtesy Beverly Hills Hotel)*

ceived, overfinanced, and badly cast motion pictures.

A Deal Is Born Deals can be launched in a number of ways. These are as follows:

1. A deal can be generated when a producer, director, or actor buys an option on a piece of writing (a property) such as a novel, short story, article, script, or treatment.

2. A producer, actor, or director can start a deal by coming up with an original notion for a motion picture and hiring a writer to work it through the usual stages. The usual stages are notion, idea, concept, outline, treatment, and script.

3. A writer can start a deal by pitching an idea to a producer or studio exec. If the Movers and Shakers are grabbed by the idea, they may hire the writer to take it through development.

When any part of a deal is consummated (i.e., the contracts are actually signed), people start making money. The screenwriter gets paid in increments to develop the script; the producer gets a fee from the studio for developing the script. Others may also get development fees. Unfortunately, only once in a blue moon does a deal make it to the screen. Most are shelved during development. By some estimates only one out of every one hundred deals makes it to principle photography.

A Friend in Need Deals that go through with relative ease are usually the ones made by old cronies among themselves. Hollywood is a small club and the members generally prosper. To illustrate, imagine that a producer has an original idea for a motion picture. The producer is represented by an agent who also represents some name talent looking for a vehicle. The agent, of course, is chummy with the studio exec, as is the producer. So what happens? The agent takes a meeting with the producer in a local sauna. They discuss the idea. The agent offers his name talent, a name writer and a name director; the producer says okay; and they both take the package to their old pal the studio exec, who offers them a hefty development deal. The screenwriter makes money developing the script; the producer gets a fee from the studio; and the agent gets a packaging fee. Everyone is happy.

Where the Elite Usually Meet Meetings can be taken anywhere, not just in the Polo Lounge or in someone's studio office. Here are just a few of Hollywood's favorite meeting places:
1. Jacuzzis
2. Men's hair salons (some have handy phone jacks)
3. Parties, weddings, bar mitzvahs, screenings, premieres, and funerals.
4. Cannes
5. Palm Springs
6. Tennis courts and golf courses
7. Health clubs, saunas, and steamrooms

☆

Deal-making Schmooze

As with any other business, the movie industry has its own quaint terminology. Although Yiddish may figure prominently in the behind-the-scenes argumentative stages of any contract negotiation (i.e., "You can take your *ferkockta* five grand and shove it up your *tuchis*, you two-bit *gonif!*"), deal-making schmooze is, for the most part, as bland and unexciting as most other forms of corporate vocabulary. Nonetheless, it is always a good idea to at least know what you're talking about in Hollywood. If nothing else, being conversant in the language of deal-making will give others the impression that you've been around.

Contract Memo A rough draft of the basic points of a contract. This stage usually precedes the contract stage.

Creative Differences The usual reason given by the publicity department for an aborted deal ("The project has been postponed due to creative differences.") Simply put, creative differences mean the director would like to strangle the producer and vice versa.

Development Deal A deal in which the studio pays a producer a fee to develop a property toward the goal of becoming a motion picture. Development usually means the writing, rewriting, and eventual shelving of a project.

Option Usually a year's lease on a property (script or book). During this period the optioner has the right to treat the optionee like an indentured servant.

Packaging An attempt by a producer or agent to make a film project more appealing by first getting a name director, name actor and name writer attached to the project before presenting it to the studio exec.

Pay-or-Play A rare contract clause in which an actor is promised his fee even if the project doesn't reach principle photography.

Pitch A peculiar literary exercise in which a screenwriter voluntarily makes a fool of himself in front of a producer by verbally explaining the plot of an unwritten script. The idea is to get the producer to agree to fund the writing of the screenplay.

Points Hollywood's quaint version of profit sharing; a percentage of the film's profits, offered to actors, directors, and/or writers as an incentive. Points can be very beneficial if: (a) the film is actually made and released, and (b) the studio decides to honor its agreement. Unfortunately, the odds of either (a) or (b) happening are about one thousand to one against.

Principle Photography That hallowed day when the cameras actually start rolling; more importantly, the day most of the people involved in the original deal receive the lion's share of their fee. If a deal actually

"According to Marty, we're not exactly divorced—we're in turnaround."

reaches the principle photography stage, it is considered a small miracle.

Rewrite What generally happens to a script when more than one ego becomes involved. The more egos, the more rewrites.

Step Deal A deal involving several predetermined stages, giving the contractor the opportunity to pull out at any stage. Steps usually involve outline, treatment, first draft, rewrite, etc.

Treatment A brief synopsis of a proposed script. The treatment follows the outline but precedes the first draft.

Turnaround When a studio's option on a project fails to get renewed, the project is said to be "in turnaround." This generally means another studio is free to pick up the option.

☆

The Evolution of a Movie

Filmmaking has so many labyrinthine stages that it is a small miracle that any films are ever released. In fact, most film projects die prior to pre-pro, but only after the principles have made enough money to spend a month in Cannes. Here are some of the general stages in a film's evolution:

Conceptual Stage A project starts with a *notion*, then an *idea*, before evolving into a *concept*, then onward to the *pitch session*. If a writer has a notion, he might take a meeting with his agent to see if it's worth working into an idea. If so, the agent will try to interest a producer and set up a meeting for the writer to pitch the concept. If the producer wants to pursue it and likes the writer, we have a deal.

Writing Once the deal is made, the writer takes the concept and works it into an *outline*, a *treatment*, then a *first draft script*, and *rewrite* until the producer finds it worthy of circulation. After a certain point the producer usually has the right to change writers without consulting the original author.

Development The producer can either try for a *development deal* with a studio, in which case those involved usually get studio offices, studio parking spaces, and fees. Or the producer can attempt to get independent financing and later hit the studios for a distribution deal after the film is shot.

Packaging In this stage, which usually comes prior to a development deal, the producer or agent tries to get name talent to commit to the project on the basis of the script. (Naturally, agents try to get as many of their *own* clients involved as possible.) This process usually involves a great deal of meeting-taking and lunch-doing in order to persuade others that the property is hot. Once a few big names have attached themselves to a project, the producer has bargaining power. He'll have an easier time getting a studio to back it or, if he's going after indie financing, he'll have more credibility. Inves-

tors tend to be easily swayed if a big name is mentioned in connection with a project.

Pre-Pro The producer puts together all the loose ends during this phase. The script is polished; the minor roles are cast; the crew is hired; the screenwriter is replaced; locations are scouted; schedules and budgets are honed, etc. Once a film gets to pre-pro it is difficult to turn back, though it has been known to happen.

Production The film is shot, usually in two months. This is the stage in which the budget is violated, the schedule is ignored, the actors tamper with dialogue, and the director comes close to experiencing a nervous breakdown.

Post-Production The footage is edited, mixed, scored, looped, and generally made presentable. At one point the finished or partially finished film is screened for the studio execs. If they like what they see, marketing plans and publicity schemes are drawn up. If they don't, the film can be shelved, sold exclusively to cable television, or opened with minimum embarrassment at "selected theaters." In the last case the press is generally not invited to screenings for fear of bad reviews. When this happens, however, word usually manages to circulate through town that the film is a turkey.

Sneak Preview A studio will sometimes hold sneak previews of a soon-to-be-released film in order to sample audience reaction early and cater publicity plans accordingly. This usually happens when the execs are insecure about the film's potential or aren't quite sure how to market it. Audiences are asked to fill out lengthy questionnaires concerning their reactions to the film and the studio marketing execs take it from there.

Distribution Exhibitors (theater-owners) bid on the

film. Some actually get to see it prior to making a bid; others don't. "Blind-bidding" is the term used to denote the process involved for those who don't.

Premiere and Release If the filmmakers have high hopes for the film, a gala premiere will be held for maximum publicity. These are occasions where paparazzi are not chased away; they are, in fact, invited. Many members of the press are even offered junkets, though this never influences their opinions and is, of course, not meant to. A week or so following the premiere the film is released, sometimes only in Los Angeles and New York (to get the major reviews), then nationwide. After the film is released the studio execs check the figures daily and hope the film has a good opening week, followed by "legs," (i.e., consistently high box-office receipts).

The Anatomy of a Movie Deal
A 3-D Horror Film

FADE IN

EXTERIOR—SUNSET BOULEVARD—DAY

Traffic is—as usual—hopelessly tied up, but everyone is too laid-back to notice. An eerie brown smog hangs over the area. Everyone seems to be driving a Mercedes 380SL, although there are a few Rolls Corniches here and there.

ANGLE—AN OFFICE BUILDING

Parked outside is a bright red 380SL with license plate spelling: MOOLAH.

CLOSE-UP—SIGN ON BUILDING

The sign is: CHEAPSHOT PRODUCTIONS LTD.

ANGLE—THE NARRATOR

The spitting image of Rod Serling, he addresses us from beside the building that houses Cheapshot Productions.

> NARRATOR ·
> Sunset Boulevard. Inside this very
> building, an independent producer
> named Murray Dreck has come up
> with an original idea for a motion
> picture, an idea so horrible,
> hundreds of innocent people will
> suffer before it is put to rest.

INTERIOR—A PLUSH OFFICE—DAY

As the camera pans around the room we hear the voices of Murray Dreck, the producer, and his director of creative development (i.e., secretary) Kate Kibitz. They are having a story conference. As they confer the camera moves slowly around the office, stopping on such mementos as a photo of Murray shaking hands with Wayne Newton and a garish poster of a past Cheapshot production called *Bite My Face Off*.

ANGLE—MURRAY

He is your typical indie prod, in his fifties but struggling to look younger. A gold coke spoon dangles from his neck; a cheap toupee dangles from his head. His shirt is opened one button too many and his Gucci-loafered feet are propped up on his desk. He sniffles.

ANGLE—KATE

In her mid twenties, attractive but sensibly dressed. This is a career girl, who has an MFA in film from UCLA where she majored in Albanian cinema of the 1920s. She got this job by being Murray's accountant's niece.

> KATE
> (fawningly)
> I love it, Murray. I just love it!

> MURRAY
> You think you love it now,
> sweetheart, wait till you hear it. I
> mean, we're talking a high-concept
> picture; we're talking name talent;
> we're talking studio deal.

> KATE
> I'm just absolutely dying to hear it,
> Murray. *Dying.*

Murray stands up. He is getting ready to make his pitch. He waits a suspenseful beat.

                    MURRAY
The concept just came to me over
the weekend. I was sitting in the
pool, looking up at the sky, when all
of a sudden it hit me. I'll give it to
you in three words. . .
            (Pauses for effect)
A talking cat.

Kate contemplates for a moment as Murray watches her
closely for reaction.

                    KATE
A talking cat. Of course! It's
brilliant, Murray. Fantabulous! I just
absolutely love it to death! Wow. I
just can't believe the way your mind
works!

                    MURRAY
And that's only the half of it, babe.
How's this for casting—Streisand
and Beatty as the cat owners and
Richie Pryor as the cat's voice!

                    KATE
What a direction to take, Murray!
It's perfecto for them. I'm totally
blown away.

                                        CUT TO

EXTERIOR—PARAMOUNT STUDIOS—DAY

Lots of Mercedes 380SLs driving in and out of the lot.

ANGLE—A PARKING SPACE ON LOT

We focus on a new Corniche with license plate spelling:
MEL

INTERIOR—STUDIO OFFICE

Mel Macher, the studio exec, is on the phone, talking to
Murray. They are old friends, having both started as
William Morris agents ten years before.

> MEL
> (feigning enthusiasm)
> I love it, Murray. It's terrif. Of course
> I mean it. (He yawns.) Would I kid ya
> kid? Look, get Marty Gelt at Morris
> to talk package and we'll talk deal.
> Okay? Ciao, babe.

CUT TO

EXTERIOR—THE WILLIAM MORRIS AGENCY—DAY

Many Mercedes 380SLs are parked outside.

INTERIOR—A WILLIAM MORRIS OFFICE

Marty Gelt is on the phone. He seems to have a cold, for
he, too, is sniffling. Beside him on his desk is a six-foot-
tall stack of unreturned pink message slips.

> MARTY
> (feigning enthusiasm)
> It's hot, Murray baby, hot! Mel's high
> on it, too, eh? Yeah, Barbra, Warren,
> and Richie are a nice combo, but
> we're gonna need a script before I
> approach them. Have I got a writer?
> What am I, a schlemiel? 'Course I
> got a writer! His name is . . . (leafs
> randomly through messages) . . .
> Sidney Schlockmeister. He's perfecto
> for this project. His credits? His last

picture was *Stick It in Your Ear,*
which, as you know, brought in some
nice receipts for Fox last year. Sure,
I'll set up a meeting. Have your girl
call my girl, okay? Okay. Ciao.

DISSOLVE TO

CLOSE-UP—*THE HOLLYWOOD REPORTER,* PAGE 3—
DAY

Hank Grant's lead item reads: INDIE PROD MURRAY
DRECK NABS STREISAND, BEATTY, AND PRYOR FOR
TALKING FELINE EPIC. PAR TO DISTRIB.

CUT TO

INTERIOR—MURRAY DRECK'S OFFICE—DAY

Murray, wearing bright red jogging suit and eating take-
out alfalfa sprouts, is taking a meeting with Sidney
Schlockmeister. Sidney wears blue jeans, Adidas running
shoes, and a Polo shirt.

SIDNEY
(insincerely)
I love the idea, Mr. Dreck. It's got
real . . . social value.

MURRAY
(with mouth full)
Call me Murray. We already got
Paramount, not to mention
Streisand, Beatty, and Pryor. Richie
and I are (holds up two fingers) like
this.

<pre>
                    SIDNEY
         I see it as a poignant commentary on
         the times. The cat sees life as it
         really is. I see it as very
         Runyonesque.

                    MURRAY
                (with mouth full)
         I know where you're coming from,
         Sid. Onionesque is exactly what I
         had in mind. We really think alike
         (looks at his watch). Oops. Got a
         meeting over at the Dôme and I'm
         already running late. Gotta run.
</pre>

Sidney gets up to leave, searching Murray's face for some sign that he's got a deal. Murray's face, however, is characteristically blank as he puts an arm around Sidney and walks him to the door.

<pre>
                    MURRAY
         You're a great talent, Sid, and a
         beautiful guy. Let's have lunch soon
         and talk plot.
</pre>

Sidney exits, looking somewhat crestfallen. He's heard that before.

CUT TO

MONTAGE—SERIES OF SHOTS

1. Sidney paces nervously in front of his phone, which is annoyingly dormant.
2. Murray is taking a meeting with other writers in his office, going through exactly the same sequence as with Sidney.
3. Back to Sidney pacing in front of phone

CUT TO

INTERIOR—HOLLYWOOD PARTY—NIGHT

A chic Hollywood get-together. Everyone drinks Perrier. Starlets abound. We locate Sidney in the crowd, talking to a starlet.

>   SIDNEY
>   (casually)
>   Actually, I got a deal pending to
>   write Murray Dreck's new picture for
>   Paramount.
>
>   STARLET
>   Gee, you think there'd be a part for
>   me?
>
>   SIDNEY
>   Sure, sweetheart. I'll see what I can
>   do. Murray and I are (holds up two
>   fingers) like this.

CUT TO

INTERIOR—SIDNEY'S HOUSE—DAY

Sidney is still pacing in front of his phone. Finally, he breaks down, picks it up, and dials his agent, Marty Gelt.

CUT TO

INTERIOR—MARTY GELT'S OFFICE

Marty's secretary picks up the ringing phone.

>   SECRETARY
>   Hold on, Sidney. (She buzzes Marty.)
>   Marty, are you in for Sidney

Schlockmeister? (Back to Sidney.)
I'm sorry, Sidney, he's in a meeting.
Of course I'll tell him it's urgent. Yes,
I know you've already left seventy-
six messages, but he's been very very
busy. 'Bye.

CUT TO

INTERIOR—SIDNEY'S HOUSE

Sidney slams down the receiver, exasperated.

CUT TO

INTERIOR—POLO LOUNGE—THE FOLLOWING
WEEK

Sidney is having a drink with his agent, Marty Gelt.

> MARTY
> Of course I'm sure you got the deal.
> Murray loves your approach to the
> material. He wants an outline first,
> then a treatment and a first draft. I
> think we can get you about twenty
> big ones and a hundred more on
> principle photography.

> SIDNEY
> (relieved)
> You're a great agent, Marty. Sorry I
> screamed at you last week. I didn't
> mean that stuff about firebombing
> your 380SL.

> MARTY
> It's all water under the bridge, Sid.
> You're hot now, babe. I think you're

really gonna go places now, kid. The
sky's the limit. We're talking serious
points on your next picture. We're
talking name director. We're talking
. . .

                                        CUT TO

MONTAGE—SEQUENCE OF SHOTS

Sidney and Murray are working together on the script.
Murray gives his creative input, while Sidney types draft
after draft.

                    MURRAY
            We need a food fight in there
            somewhere, Sid. And a couple of
            chase scenes—real heavy
            destruction. And the love story needs
            more pizzazz, and . . .

As he types frenetically, Sidney rolls his eyes. The
narrator steps out of the office closet as all of this is going
on.

                    NARRATOR
            Though Sidney writes three versions
            of the script, Murray keeps sending
            him back for revisions. While Sidney
            writes, Murray sees to the casting . . .

                                        CUT TO

INTERIOR—MA MAISON—NIGHT

Murray is having a drink with a starlet. She is, to put it
mildly, robust in certain areas. Murray periodically waves
to someone at another table to impress her.

                    STARLET
You really think I'd be right for the
part, Mr. Dreck?

                                        CUT TO

EXTERIOR—MURRAY'S JACUZZI—NIGHT

Through the thick hot cloud of chlorine steam, we can
just make out the faces of Murray and his starlet.

                                        CUT TO

INTERIOR—MURRAY'S OFFICE—LATER THAT
MONTH

Sidney, his eyes bloodshot, watches expectantly as Murray
reads the script. The title page is: "CAT GOT YOUR
TONGUE—SIXTH DRAFT." Finally, Murray puts it down.

                    MURRAY
I love it, Sid. You're a great talent.

                    SID
                (relieved)
I couldn't have done it without your
creative input, Murray.

                    MURRAY
I only got one little problem, pal. You
wrote it for Streisand and Beatty.

                    SID
You told me . . .

                    MURRAY
I know, but I had a change of mind.
It came to me last night in a vision.
It suddenly occurred to me that this

picture is too highbrow—it's got no
appeal to the kids. Streisand and
Beatty are all wrong for this picture.

                    SIDNEY
But . . .

                    MURRAY
What this picture needs is some
young talent—Brooke Shields and
John Travolta maybe. We'll keep
Richie Pryor and get the black
audience, too. This picture is gonna
be a monster, kid. A monster!

ANGLE—SIDNEY

He is crying. The thought of a seventh draft has taken its
toll. The narrator steps out of the closet.

                    NARRATOR
A few weeks pass. Murray gets
another writer to rewrite the script
for Brooke Shields and John Travolta.
Shields and Travolta commit to the
project and Murray moves to the
Paramount lot.

                                        CUT TO

EXTERIOR—PARAMOUNT PARKING SPACE—DAY

A Corniche with license plate MOOLAH is parked in front
of a backlot office. The name Murray Dreck is being
painted on the space.

INTERIOR—MURRAY'S PARAMOUNT OFFICE

Murray sits at his desk reading *Variety*. He is still sniffling.

ANGLE—*VARIETY*

The headline is: PAR V.P. MEL MACHER MOVES TO
FOX. Murray reads the headline and falls off his chair.

CUT TO

EXTERIOR—MURRAY'S OLD OFFICE ON SUNSET
BOULEVARD—DAY

Murray's old 380SL is parked in front. (He has returned
the Corniche.)

INTERIOR—MURRAY'S OLD OFFICE

Murray is sitting at his desk and still sniffling. His copy of
CAT GOT YOUR TONGUE is stacked amid other scripts
on the shelf. Kate and Murray are having another story
conference.

> KATE
> I love it, Murray. I just love it!

> MURRAY
> You think you love it now, wait till
> you hear it.
>
> I'll give it to you in four words. . . .
> (Pauses for effect)
> Hamsters from outer space!

> KATE
> I love it, Murray! It's brilliant! What
> a direction to take. It's . . .

ANGLE—NARRATOR

He appears from under the desk.

NARRATOR

And so the tragic story ends. Murray is back in his old office. Kate is starting to call her contacts to see if she can get another job, perhaps at one of the studios. Mel Macher is rising fast at Fox. The two starlets are meeting a lot of producers. Marty Gelt has left the Morris Agency to become a vice-president at Paramount. And Sidney Schlockmeister is spending a few months at a sanitorium in Oregon.

FADE OUT

PART THREE

The Status Game

☆☆☆☆☆☆☆☆☆☆☆☆☆☆☆☆☆☆☆☆☆

The Right Stuff

*"There are only two kinds of class—
first class and no class."*
—David O. Selznick

For the most part, film-making involves the creation of illusions and images through the clever use of special effects, backdrops, facades, and the like. Robert Redford seems to be walking down a turn-of-the-century New York street, but he's actually just strolling along a studio backdrop of well-crafted facades. The Shangri-la we think we see glittering in the distance is actually nothing more than a very realistic painting superimposed on blank film. Fake blood spurts, actors grow old in an hour's time, werewolves sprout hair before our eyes. It all looks and feels real, but it is nothing more than well-constructed fakery. Such is the wonder and magic of filmmaking.

Unfortunately, Hollywood has gone one step beyond and made the practice of well-crafted fakery a preferred lifestyle. Everyone is an actor playing a role, and images are created through the special effects of status. In Hollywood every person is the producer, writer, director, costume designer, makeup artist, and special-effects technician of his own life, and it better not be a low-budget production, either. If, as Shakespeare wrote, all the world's a stage, in Hollywood it is a big screen brought to you in Dolby sound.

Granted, you'd be hard-pressed to find a part of the country that doesn't go in for status symbols and the accoutrements of success, but

Hollywood has managed to crystallize status-seeking into a mania. All other aspects of life take a backseat, preferably one in a Rolls Corniche. In Hollywood not only must you drive the right car, you must be seen at all the right places, with the right people, all of you wearing the right clothes. And you must know at least one maître d' by name, live at the proper address, patronize the right chiropractor, go to the right health club, and be in possession of an unlisted phone number. Going to the right psychiatrist, psychic, hairdresser, and plastic surgeon can't hurt, either.

Real street or studio backdrop?

☆

You Are What You Drive

According to popular mythology a major American oil company in cahoots with a major American car manufacturer contrived years ago to squelch city plans to construct an ambitious public transportation system for Greater Los Angeles, thus ensuring the future of oil and car sales in the area. Though lately the joke seems to be on them—oil prices are faltering and the American car has become déclassé—the effort has paid off. Los Angeles is still the most automobile-oriented metropolis in America. There *are* buses, but only honest, working people take them. Movie people drive.

The automobile is the single most visible status symbol of success Hollywood has to offer. The effect of an expensive car in Hollywood should never be underestimated; it is, quite simply, essential to be seen driving a vehicle that costs roughly what a normal person would consider a reasonable down payment for a three-bedroom house. The studio exec with anything less than a Mercedes 380SL adorning his personal parking space may very well find his colleagues declining to meet him for lunch. Pulling up at a gala premiere in anything lower than a limo, Rolls, or Bentley usually results in derisive laughter. Even the valets at Ma Maison will have serious second thoughts about creasing their uniforms on the cheap vinyl seats of anything as pedestrian as a Datsun 280Z.

Maximum Prestige Private limos, Rolls-Royces, and Bentleys represent the peak of achievement in Hollywood. Those seen driving or riding in one of these vehicles—especially behind smoked windows—evoke natural curiosity and reverence in passers-by. Naturally, size and rarity of these models is a significant factor. Even the Rolls Corniche has become almost too common to have much effect in Hollywood. It is the Rollses and Bentleys that look like they were once used

The Mighty Rolls

The Mogul's Mercedes

**The Posh
Porsche**

to transport English royalty to the coronation that get the real attention nowadays. The Corniche is merely standard equipment for studio heads and stars.

The Mercedes Though Rollses and Bentleys abound, the Mercedes 380SL is by far the most popular automotive status symbol on the road. If the rest of the world banned the sale of the 380SL, Mercedes-Benz would still turn a handsome profit just supplying Hollywood. Even those with Rollses and Bentleys will keep a couple of 380SLs for the kiddies or in which to run errands. The one danger the 380SL has encountered is that its very overpopularity has corroded its effect as a status symbol—it has become standard equipment. The Mercedes 380SL is favored largely by high-level agents, TV writers, directors and producers.

The Jaunty Jag

The Up-and-Coming BMW

BMW, Excalibur, Jaguar, Porsche Running a close second to Mercedes and catching up fast is the BMW. Many Hollywoodians, sensing that the 380SL has overstayed its welcome as a status car, but still possessed of an overwhelming need to drop thirty grand on a German automobile, are opting for top-of-the-line BMWs. The BMW is irrefutably a nice car but it is *not* a Mercedes, and Mercedes owners will be the first to let you know it. Moreover, the Bavarian Motor Works doesn't make convertibles yet—if they ever do, the Mercedes might be in real trouble. The BMW is considered a nice car for comers such as studio veeps, screenwriters, and rising directors of development, but, chances are most of them will trade it in for a 380SL when they move up that critical notch.

The Porsche has maintained a fairly consistent fringe popularity for the last five or ten years. In the late seventies it seemed as if everyone was suddenly buying a Porsche, and the car had a two-year surge in popularity during this period. Nowadays it is still popular with real car enthusiasts, although, as any 380SL owner will be quick to point out, it isn't a Mercedes.

One can still spot an occasional Excalibur or Clenet on the streets, but these are generally considered to be too showy and attract more attention from tourists than Hollywood veterans. The same goes for DeLoreans, now that the drug-bust sensation has ebbed. Jaguars are popular among those who also have Rollses and Bentleys and find it convenient to communicate in English with their mechanic. The Jag's prestige rating has dropped off slightly in recent years.

American Cars Cadillacs are still popular among old-line Hollywood agents and producers who can afford to moor them. Mustang convertibles, if rare and well kept, have a certain status appeal. But, generally speaking, American models are totally déclassé. Stay away from Corvettes and Trans Ams—these are for local high-school kids, the 'Vette being a long-time favorite of the Orange County debutante. Pickup trucks are also out.

Miscellaneous Wheels No prestige whatsoever will be gained from driving a Saab, Volvo, Datsun, Toyota, Audi, Honda, Peugeot, or Fiat. These are sensible cars that get good gas mileage and have reasonable maintenance costs. These factors alone contrive to make them low on the prestige scale. After all, who wants to own a car that doesn't cost a fortune to maintain?

☆☆☆☆☆☆ THE CAR STATUS SCALE ☆☆☆☆☆☆

Make	Status Factor
Rolls, Bentley, Limo	10
Mercedes	9
Jag, Porsche, BMW	7
DeLorean, Clenet, Domestic Collector's Car	5
Used BMW, Mercedes, Porsche, Jag, Bentley	4
Cadillac, Peugeot, Audi, Mazda	3
Honda, Toyota, Datsun, Rabbit, American Domestic Car	2
Corvette, Trans Am, VW Bug, Le Car, Pickup	0

THE RIGHT STUFF ★ 124

☆ ☆ ☆ ☆ ☆ ☆ **ROLLS VS. MERCEDES**   ☆ ☆ ☆ ☆ ☆ ☆

One of the more pressing problems confronting many in
Hollywood is trying to decide when to take the Rolls and when to
take the Mercedes. It is a question equal in philosophical import to
such quandaries as, "What shall I wear?" and "Where shall we
eat?" Here are a few pointers for those fortunate enough to have
this problem:

Car	Destination
Rolls	Ma Maison, Chasen's, Rodeo Drive, benefits, premieres, studios, Polo Lounge, bank, studio exec's house, Beverly Hills parties, funerals, weddings, Palm Springs

| Mercedes | Le Dôme, Musso's, tax audit, Westwood, the Marina, UCLA, Santa Monica, your agent's house for dinner, a movie screening, Melrose Avenue, Mexico |

☆ ☆

Poetic License

In Hollywood it is not always enough to drive the right car. After all, *anyone* can buy a Rolls or a 380SL, even those not involved in show biz. The personalized license plate can be used to identify you from the masses of ordinary citizens by spelling out your profession, your general attitude toward life or the depth of your affluence in seven letters or less. These often cryptic self-promotional signs are a vivid testimony to the uncanny cleverness of Hollywoodians. Here are a few existing examples:

LUV CASH	LOADED	AGENT
SLEAZE	MONYBGS	BUCKSSS
WRITOR	PEE DOC	VID KID
EDITOR	MR BIG	STARLET
GELT	I HEAL	TV KID
MOOLAH	BIGTIME	MOGUL

Hollywood Lore

Upon leaving a posh Hollywood restaurant one evening, Frank Sinatra handed his parking stub to a waiting valet. A few seconds later the valet returned with the car.

"What's the biggest tip you ever got?" Sinatra asked.

"One hundred dollars, sir," the valet replied.

"I'll top that," Sinatra said. "Here's two hundred."

The valet accepted the bills graciously and Sinatra climbed into his car. As an afterthought, Sinatra asked, "By the way, who gave you the hundred?"

"You did, sir," the valet said.

☆

The All-important Address

The Hollywood Hills—a Status Address

If you are at a party and the person with whom you are conversing over chilled glasses of Perrier with lime has not had the overwhelming thrill of seeing what kind of car you drive, chances are he or she will attempt to classify you on the status scale by asking where you live. The continuation of the relationship may very well depend on your reply.

First of all, do not be put off by the query. It is fairly common in Hollywood society and should not be interpreted as a blatant request for an invitation to your place, even if asked by a member of the opposite sex. It should be interpreted for what it is—a veiled request to ascertain how much money you make.

Before discussing your reply, it is important to talk real estate. Los Angeles, often described as a city of suburbs, is made up of several hundred square miles of different residential communities. Beverly Hills, Santa Monica, Westwood, and Encino are a few of these areas. Each area has its own specific connotations in terms of the wealth and prosperity of its inhabitants. Moreover, it is no secret that real-estate prices in all of the Southland are sky high.

With those two factors in mind, how do you choose an address that will have some meaning yet not put you in debt? To begin with, it doesn't really matter at all *where* you live—what matters is only where you *say* you live. Malibu, Bel Air, Beverly Hills, and Hollywood Hills are all top-notch addresses. Westwood and Santa Monica, along with the Sherman Oaks Hills and Toluca Lake, are fair to middling. Never say you live in Burbank, Van Nuys, or Studio City, which is the Valley, a connotation that will result in immediate condescension. Although the concept of the "Valley Girl" has received some nationwide attention recently, it is not considered a plus to admit to being one.

In Hollywood it is never enough to simply name the area in which you reside. You must, in these situations, convey the information that you *own* a house and that it comes with one or more of the following features:

1. Tennis court
2. Screening room
3. Game room
4. Racquetball or squash court
5. Jacuzzi
6. Exercise room

Obviously, combinations of any of these elements will raise your status proportionately. If you have all six, you have arrived. Naturally, you can't come right out and say, "I own a twelve-bedroom mansion in Beverly Hills with tennis court, screening room, game room, squash court, Jacuzzi, and exercise room." That would be transparent. It is better to be convincingly subtle, such as, "It's so difficult to get responsible poolmen these days," or "My squash court floor buckled during the last rain storm," or "My Jacuzzi flooded my guest house."

The Address Status Scale

Address	Status Factor
Bel Air, Beverly Hills, Malibu	10
Any Canyon	9
Hollywood Hills	8
Santa Monica, the Marina	7
Beverly Hills adjacent	6
Westwood	5
Sherman Oaks Hills, Encino South	4
North Hollywood, Studio City	3
Venice	2
Van Nuys	0

☆

Name-dropping: Novice, Intermediate, and Advanced

Clout by association is an integral part of the Hollywood status game. You will be judged in terms of the friends you claim to have, so naturally it is wise to claim to have friends whose names ring bells, the louder the better.

Name-dropping has become something of an art form in Hollywood. Just knowing the right names to drop is certainly a prerequisite, but it is only half the battle. One must also know *how* to drop them, in what contexts and in what prevailing attitude.

To begin with, always use first names whenever possible. Hollywood is a relaxed, casual place in which everyone is immediately on a first-name basis. Jack Nicholson and Anjelica Huston, for example, would be referred to simply as Jack and Anjelica. When discussing a person with a common first name, use the last name *once* as identification, then resume discussion using only the first name. Use nicknames whenever possible, as in Bob Redford and Dusty Hoffman.

Never admit that you don't know someone whose name has been dropped. Always say yes if someone says to you, "I was doing lunch with Bob Mitchum last week—you know Bob, don't you?" In Hollywood if you've heard of someone, you *know* him.

Always refer to the person whose name has been dropped as a friend. Everyone in Hollywood is a friend—no one is an acquaintance or associate.

Casualness is the key ingredient for delivery. Never force an occasion to name-drop; always work it in as subtly as possible. Being too obvious about it will only compromise your credibility. And don't overdo it—two names per conversation is the usual limit.

The Name-dropping Status Scale

Name	Status Factor
Superstar, powerful entertainment lawyer, William Morris agent, studio head, Rolls-Royce dealer, owner of top-ten restaurant, president of network programming, Frank Sinatra, George Lucas, President of the United States	10
Star, ICM or CAA agent, studio veep, major producer or director, network programming veep, German-car mechanic, top-ten maître d', Beverly Hills shrink, governor	8
TV star, studio veep for creative development, rock star, major drug dealer, sitcom producer, head of daytime TV programming, mayor	6
Screenwriter, commercial director, top-ten waiter, Japanese-car mechanic, studio story editor, William Morris receptionist, studio gate guard, guru, David Begelman's hair stylist	2

Status Spiel #1

"Patrick[1] brought Warren and Diane[2] over to our table at Maison[3] last night. Their *saumon en croûte*[4] is absolutely to *die* for! And what a coincidence! We discovered that Diane's agent—you know Marty[5], don't you?—is a close friend of Fritz[6], my mechanic!"

Footnotes
1. Patrick Terrail, owner of Ma Maison
2. Warren Beatty and Diane Keaton (still friends)
3. Poshest joint in town: Ma Maison
4. Great and popular dish
5. Standard Morris agent
6. Mercedes mechanic

"We were supposed to go to the Emmys but we couldn't decide whether to take the Rolls or the Bentley so we stayed home."

Status Spiel #2

"Last weekend I was shopping on the Drive[1] when Giorgio[2] told me they were towing my 380[3]. Well, it *was* parked in a handicapped zone[4]. I would have valet-parked it but the 380 *is* almost a year old and the Rolls[5] is in the shop. Anyway, just as they were hiking it up, who walks by but Jon and Barb[6]. Thank God! Jon managed to talk the towers out of it, since I was parked in front of his salon, and I was so grateful I asked them to dinner at Chows[7].

Footnotes
1. Rodeo Drive
2. The usual Italian couturier
3. Mercedes 380SL
4. Beverly Hills noblesse oblige
5. Rolls-Royce
6. Jon Peters and Barbra Streisand
7. Mr. Chows

Where to Be Seen

Eating at the right restaurants, drinking at the right bars, shopping at the right stores, even *atoning* at the right synagogues is a key element in the Hollywood status game. By definition, the right places are those habituated by Hollywood's upper echelon—the ones who make the right places right. After all, no one hangs out at the Polo Lounge simply because the bartender mixes a superior Perrier with lime.

Restaurants and Bars Although Hollywood has a few perennial "in" spots (notably Ma Maison, the Polo Lounge, and Chasen's), new trendy restaurants and bars seem to spring up out of nowhere with disconcerting regularity. Naturally, it is important to be able to keep up with the latest hangouts. The question is, how?

Basically, Hollywood's version of a trendy restaurant has the following five elements in common:

1. Unlisted phone number
2. Front parking lot full of Rolls-Royces
3. Small portions for high prices
4. Foreign-accented maître d' from central casting
5. Celebrity backers

Unfortunately, anyone—even tourists—are allowed to go to trendy restaurants to dine. The patron who wants to be regarded as a "regular," must stand out from the crowd. This is accomplished in the following three ways:

1. Knowing the maître d' or owner
2. Keeping up on the restaurant's menu
3. Getting the best table

Maître D' or Owner The owner of Ma Maison is Patrick Terrail. To get the names of other owners and maître d's, simply call the restaurant (if you can get the phone number) before you go and ask for names. When you arrive at the restaurant,

make like the maître d' or owner served with you in the French resistance.

Dishes Here is another head start: a few of Le Dôme's most popular dishes are the cold duck salad and the swordfish with anchovy butter. To learn more, call ahead and ask for a recital of the menu. When you arrive, wax rhapsodic about the joint's absolutely sumptuous salmon mousse with leeks.

Getting the Best Table Merely being in possession of the small fortune required to pay the average restaurant bill in Holly-wood is not enough. Status means securing the best table in the place. Every Hollywood "in" spot has a best table, generally the one located in the area to which the other patrons' eyes are most naturally directed. Dining at this beknighted spot means you are someone worth gawking at.

Securing the best table in a top-ten eatery is a contest that ought to someday become an Olympic event. They usually go to stars, directors, producers, or studio execs. Most restaurateurs are on a first-name basis with these people and know them on sight.

If you are a relative unknown desirous of obtaining the best table, scamming it is your only hope. Try this tactic: call the maître d', explain that you are (choose one): the private secretary of a Saudi sheik, *Gourmet* magazine food critic, or local director of the Internal Revenue Service.

Shopping The only place to be seen shopping is Rodeo Drive. Prices here run the gamut from outrageous to unreasonable but, though you'd be better off actually making your purchases at J. C. Penney's, it is essential to be *seen* throwing money around on Rodeo Drive. Here are a few rules of conduct that apply for shopping on the Drive:

1. Always take your Rolls and park it next to a hydrant. The towing charge is a small price to pay for the attention.

2. Wear a jogging suit. Overdressing for Rodeo Drive signals the fact that you are either from out of town or from the Valley.

3. Always assume a snottier attitude than the sales clerks who are helping you.

4. Never let on that something is too expensive. A $1,200 pair of undershorts on Rodeo Drive is known as a bargain.

Walking and Running Since Hollywood is so car-

Being seen at the beach indicates to others that you do not have your own swimming pool.

oriented it is not considered cool to be seen walking anywhere except Rodeo Drive, Westwood, and Santa Monica. Never walk on Sunset Boulevard between Sweetzer and La Brea since this is the exclusive turf of Hollywood's ladies of the evening, most of whom seem to work both day and night. Prostitution certainly isn't legal in Hollywood but it goes on, provided it takes place at the proper areas, such as over lunch or at a story conference.

Similarly, joggers should not take to the streets since this implies the lack of suitable health club facilities. In other words, it is fine to wear a jogging suit as long as you don't jog in it.

The Beach Although the area boasts many lovely public beaches, those interested in making it in Hollywood would be well advised to steer clear of them. Your presence on a public beach betrays the fact that you don't have a swimming pool. Private beaches and moored yachts parked at the Marina are okay.

Hollywood Lore

A well-known country and western star was in Hollywood for the very first time and, on his first night, his manager asked him where he wanted to have dinner.

"Let's go to Mama's Own," the singer drawled. "I heard the food there is great."

Although the manager had never heard of Mama's Own, he assumed it would be in the phone book. It wasn't. In fact, no one the manager talked to had ever heard of a restaurant called Mama's Own.

About a week later it became clear that the country and western singer was referring to Hollywood's ritziest eatery, Ma Maison.

"Paging Mr. Selznick!"

Getting paged at the Polo Lounge is no longer the essential attention-getter it used to be—too many unknowns have abused it by setting up prearranged paging schemes with their friends. Nowadays status is having the Polo Lounge's maître d' silently bring a phone to your table *without* having to page you first.

Where to Be Seen: Restaurants

Go to . . .	If You Want to Be Seen By . . .
1. Ma Maison	Anyone who is anyone
2. Trumps	Up-and-coming Hollywood elite
3. Spago	Everybody
4. Lucy's	Paramount execs or Jerry Brown
5. Cock 'n' Bull	TV writers, producers, etc.
6. Scandia	Old-line Hollywood
7. Polo Lounge	Agents, producers, writers
8. Chasen's	Old-line Hollywood stars
9. Musso & Frank's Grill	Actors and writers who miss New York
10. Le Dôme	John Travolta, Olivia Newton-John, Rod Stewart

Dressed to Maim: The Hollywood Uniform

Needless to say, Hollywood is not one of the world's leading fashion centers. Couturiers do not travel miles upon miles to bear witness to Tinseltown's new spring line of halter tops, Hawaiian shirts, and designer jeans. Dress is stylish, but hardly earth-shattering in originality.

Although most of America sees Hollywood's glitterati in the tuxedos and designer gowns sported every spring at the Academy Award ceremonies, formal garb of this ilk is hardly the norm. In Hollywood, casual is the key; clothes are meant as an extension of the laid-back personality. If anything, Hollywoodians dress not to one-up each other, but rather to one-*down* each other, to see who can be the most casual. Consequently, blue jeans, designer and otherwise, still reign supreme. Indeed, so common and acceptable are jeans that no restaurant, no matter how chi-chi, would dare to bar entry to a jeans-wearer. And, of course, more important than jogging itself is the omnipresent jogging suit.

More important than jogging is the perennial jogging suit.

Sunglasses Shades are standard equipment in Hollywood for three reasons. First, the sun is actually out about 89.2 percent of the time, and it is a bright, garish sunlight that hurts the naked eye. Second, shades are necessary for shielding the eyes from smog, which on direct contact can cause the eyes to water relentlessly. Third, and most importantly, shades are essential for maintaining a laid-back attitude—behind shades the true expression of one's face is effectively hidden from view. With shades the mouth can be saying one thing, while the eyes say another.

The Writers' Uniform Most screenwriters generally dress alike. The standard writer's garb usually consists of faded blue jeans, Adidas running shoes, Lacoste or Polo shirt, and sports jacket. Of all the Hollywood echelons, writers are the most shabbily attired, perhaps as a reflection of the way in which they are usually treated by those who are dressed better, such as producers and studio execs.

☆

The Open-Shirt Controversy

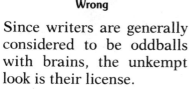

Wrong

Right

Since writers are generally considered to be oddballs with brains, the unkempt look is their license.

The Fred C. Dobbs Look The unshaven face (or Fred C. Dobbs Look) has long been a favorite of Hollywood's creative community. It signifies that the wearer is too obsessed with his creative work to have the time to engage in anything as mundane as shaving. Of course, maintaining a convincing Dobbs Look requires a great deal of grooming—one has to know how far to let the beard grow, maintaining stubble without going full force into a beard. Moreover, those sporting the Dobbs Look must keep the rest of their attire fairly neat, so as not to be mistaken for a wino.

Producers and Agents The clichéd Gucci loafer is still high on the list for producers and agents, a holdover from the old days, and still a sign of success. Rolex watches serve a similar purpose. Blue jeans are standard for new-line agents and producers, but the old line still prefers sporty dress slacks. The same goes for thick cigars. As for the clichéd open-collared-shirt, white-shoes-and-gold-chain look—that went out in the fifties, except for an occasional used-car dealer who still thinks it is a with-it way to dress. Studio execs, many of them ex-agents and ex-producers, generally keep to their former styles, which makes it difficult to identify the hierarchical differences. Three-piece suits and ties are the exclusive terrain of lawyers who still have to wear them in court.

☆

The Hollywood Lifestyle

BODY AND SOUL

Not since ancient Greece has the attention paid to mind and body been as thoroughly obsessive as it is in present-day Hollywood. (Note: In Hollywood, the term "mind" should never be confused with the term "intellect.") For some reason—be it the warm climate or the preponderance of actors—Hollywoodians feel compelled to look and feel beautiful and will spend untold amounts of money toward this end. The results are breathtaking. Hollywood has more beautiful people, more health-food fanatics, exercise classes, masseurs, chiropractors, and consciousness-raising trends than anywhere else on earth. Ironically, it also has some rather alarming statistics regarding divorce, drug abuse, and suicide.

Be that as it may, in order to gain full acceptance in Hollywood, it is mandatory to engage in some activity designed to promote health, beauty, and total heaviosity. Those who disdain such pastimes as a waste of time or profess skepticism will soon find their dance cards empty. Hollywoodians love to talk about the state of their minds and bodies at any given point in time more than anything else. The ability to utter such phrases as, "I'm starting to get in touch with my feelings," or "Bone manipulation is where it's at," with a straight face is essential in Hollywood society.

The following is a guide to what is cool and what isn't in the engaging world of health, fitness, and mind-expansion:

1. *Healers* It is imperative to have an offbeat healer of some sort, either a chiropractor, acupuncturist, holistic healer, or Amazonian witch doctor. Quote him flagrantly, as in "My neo-holistic chiropractor says diabetes can be completely cured by tapping the tibia after eating a bagel with algae." Speak of your healer in reverent tones. When encountering skepticism, simply smile beatifically as if the skeptic were a pagan idol worshipper. But don't worry too much about skeptics, as most Hollywoodians are anxious to hear new cures for old ailments. For your own safety, keep the number of a certified medical doctor but don't tell anyone about it.

2. *Shrinks* In Hollywood status rises proportionately with the number of times per week you see a shrink. Make sure it is a well-known Beverly Hills shrink. Most people in the industry suffer the usual neuroses—guilt, insecurity, etc.—but cover these up convincingly with their laid-back attitude, a practice that only serves to exacerbate the situation. When throwing a party, it is considered tasteful to invite your shrink and introduce him as your shrink. Having a status shrink at your home is like having a status car in your garage.

3. *Mind-Expansion* Always profess participation in at least one of the following activities: self-hypnosis, yoga, sensory-deprivation experiences, meditation.

The Source—a popular vegetarian restaurant

4. *Face Value* It is okay to admit to extravagant vanity. Even your average Hollywood male will spend $150 to have his hair coiffed in Beverly Hills or drop $50 at a tanning parlor. Men in Hollywood are also no strangers to facials, massages, manicures, pedicures, and plastic surgery.

5. *Fitness* Absolutely everyone in Hollywood belongs to a health club featuring either Nautilus or aerobics. To refrain from some form of organized exercise means instant pariahhood. Also considered very bad form is the ingestion of red meat and cigarettes. In Hollywood vegetarianism is practically a religion, and it is not unusual to be barred entry from a home if you smoke. It is also considered bad form to smoke while jogging, exercising, meditating, or while enclosed in a samadhi tank.

☆

Basic Hollywood Etiquette

It is part of the wonder and diversity of life on this planet that what passes for rudeness in one culture is considered the height of propriety in another. For example, in Turkey it is considered polite to belch ferociously following a satisfying repast. This gesture lets the host know that the meal was greatly appreciated. Similarly, in France the gourmet is gravely insulted if his waiter fails to treat him with the proper degree of condescension and indifference.

Hollywood has its own peculiar rules regarding correct behavior. Adhering to these can be a significant factor in rising through the ranks of Hollywood society. Here are a few fundamental do's and don'ts:

1. *DO* make sure to be late for parties, lunches, and meetings. In Hollywood, arriving late means you're busier and therefore more important than the person you're meeting. Lateness is a subtle form of hype.

2. *DON'T* return phone calls unless the caller has left at least three messages. Returning a call immediately is a dead giveaway that you are not busy, not important, and not very much in demand.

3. *DO* put all callers on hold for at least five minutes, preferably at the high point of the conversation.

4. *DON'T* attempt to bribe a maître d' at a top-ten restaurant. Seating is dependent upon reputation, not handouts.

5. *DO* use first names when addressing people, no matter how influential they may be. In Hollywood, even the Pope would be addressed as "John baby." Never say, "Sir," "Ma'am," "Mr.," "Ms.," or "Mrs.," when addressing anyone.

6. *DON'T* bad-mouth anyone or his or her projects. Bad-mouthing has a way of traveling and can subvert

THE RIGHT STUFF ★ 146

your career. In Hollywood, everyone and everything is always terrif.

7. *DO* attempt to be ingratiating to all secretaries and receptionists, particularly if they work for agents or producers. Not only do they have the power of connecting you to their bosses, they're usually related to someone important.

8. *DON'T* lay out more than two medium-sized lines when someone offers you a "toot."

9. *DO* always assume nudity when invited to take a Jacuzzi with strangers. Never wear a bathing suit or enter the water in your street clothes.

10. *DON'T* shake hands with members of the opposite sex at parties. Always kiss when being introduced even if you've never met before.

11. *DO* use the word "love," excessively, such as "I love the way your mind works," or "I love the project." In Hollywood the term "love," can mean anything.

12. *DON'T* let it be known that you smoke cigarettes, eat red meat, or disdain exercise. Further, never admit skepticism regarding psychics, holistic healers, chiropractors, and the like.

13. *DO* attempt to use at least one French word or phrase in every conversation. This signifies worldliness and taste. *Tout de suite*, *cinéma vérité*, and *avec plaisir* are all acceptable.

14. *DON'T* ask for a fork at a Japanese restaurant.

☆
Hollywood Oracles

Since success in Hollywood often seems entirely in the hands of fate, the local fortune-telling business has become quite prosperous. Producers, directors, actors, and writers, uncertain as to whether their latest deal will fall through or come to fruition, have taken to consult-

the like. It is not unusual to hear people say things like, "My psychic says the bone structure of my skull suggests that my options will always be renewed."

Naturally, psychics and astrologers and their ilk are no fools. They charge exorbitant amounts of money for the simple task of conveying optimistic fictions upon their clients who are usually only too grateful to shell out the dough, especially as most have just been informed that they will be getting a great deal *more* dough in the near future. Some even take Visa and MasterCard.

Consequently, the practice of consulting some form of seer has become an "in" thing to do in Hollywood. To save you the trouble and the expense, at the left is a reproduction of the basic Hollywood palm with all the significant lines spelled out.

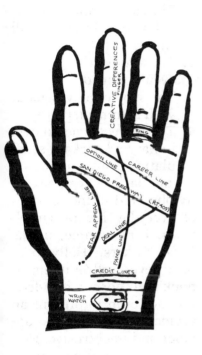

ing astrologers, palmists, psychics, tarot experts, and

☆

How to Be Truly Laid-Back

It is considered *de rigueur* in Hollywood, particularly among the industry crowd, to affect a laid-back attitude at all times. Anyone who fails to exhibit this distinctly low-key air is immediately recognized for what he is—a tourist or a recent arrival. Tourists and recent arrivals

THE RIGHT STUFF ★ 148

are seldom taken seriously unless they have significant amounts of investment capital in their portfolios or are already famous. To achieve acceptance in Hollywood without money or prior fame, it is therefore essential to be laid-back. Eastern anxieties, neuroses, and ethics are better left behind, along with snow, sleet, and a taste for good theater.

Manifestations Basically, the term "laid-back," describes a state of consciousness approximately two centimeters this side of comatose. It is the direct opposite of concepts like "expressive" and "alert." It derives, in most part, from the tropical climate, the Mexican influence, and the fact that the air Hollywoodians breathe is often lacking in elements conducive to human life.

Laid-backness manifests itself in someone in a number of identifiable ways:

1. The subject smiles frequently for no ostensible reason.
2. The subject speaks in a controlled monotone.
3. The subject wears dark glasses, even at night.
4. The subject tends to sniffle frequently.
5. The subject rolls his eyes in a jaded manner.
6. The subject affects an air of bored disinterest at all times.
7. The subject's skin is evenly tanned.
8. The subject moves about with extreme lethargy.
9. The subject is not known to have a knack for stimulating conversation.

Laid-backness can be easily observed in the routines of everyday life in Tinseltown. For example, unlike New Yorkers, Hollywoodians never yell epithets or honk their horns while driving, not even to prevent an accident. Cab drivers are quiet and unobtrusive. Hollywoodians do not argue with waiters or maître d's, nor do they make scenes in public places, speak in elevators, or have anxiety attacks in public. To be laid-back is to be cool and hip without having to try very hard. The permanent smile indicates to others a facade of peace and equanimity. The slightly bored, jaded expression demonstrates that the subject cannot be outwardly rattled by the anxieties of everyday life. Silence and monotone imply superior intelligence and understanding even though the subject may actually be dull-witted.

A totally laid-back attitude is usually achieved through one or more of the following factors:
1. Sunstroke
2. Drugs
3. Consciousness-raising
4. Hot-water immersion (Jacuzzis)
5. Vegetarianism (protein deficiency)
6. Overexertion (aerobics, etc.)

Most typical Hollywoodians achieve maximum laid-backness by engaging in all of the above activities on a fairly regular basis. This practice is commonly known as a lifestyle.

THE STATES OF LAID-BACKNESS

Laid-Back   Very Laid-Back   Deceased

——————————— ☆ ———————————

A Day in the Life of a Laid-Back Person

NAME: Marvin
PROFESSION: Producer
CAR: Mercedes 380SL
ADDRESS: Laurel Canyon
SEX: Irregular

5:30 A.M.: The radio goes off. It is set to a low-key FM station. Marvin slowly rises and chooses one of ten colorful jogging suits, all purchased on Rodeo Drive for a ridiculous price from a man named Giorgio.

5:45 A.M.: Marvin jogs down to the kitchen and prepares his morning vegetable-and-fruit drink in the food processor. (He never drinks coffee because caffeine makes one hyper, and decaffeinated coffee is carcinogenic.) The drink consists of celery, alfalfa sprouts, orange juice, wheat germ, avocado, ginseng root, sheep enzymes, gelatinous algae, and yogurt. It tastes like liquid chalk.

6:00 A.M.: Marvin jogs to his aerobics class, inhaling the brisk morning air, which, in his neighborhood, is roughly equivalent to smoking two packs of cigarettes.

6:45 A.M.: He exercises, saunas, and is massaged by a six-foot Swede who once had a role in *The Incredible Hulk*.

7:30 A.M.: He meditates for twenty minutes back at his home. His mantra is "gross points." Afterwards, he takes a ten-minute Jacuzzi. By this time, his general demeanor resembles that of an extra in *Night of the Living Dead*.

8:00 A.M.: He puts on his clothes—designer jeans, Gucci loafers, silk Armani shirt open to mid-chest, and sunglasses.

8:30 A.M.: He drives to work in his convertible Mercedes 380SL. His license plate is: LUV CASH. People behind him on the freeway feel the overwhelming urge to tailgate.

8:35 A.M.: A Mack truck cuts him off in heavy traffic, almost causing a twelve-car accident. Marvin refuses to be rattled; his low-key attitude remains intact. He smiles at the truck driver.

9:00 A.M.: He arrives at work. While he reads *Variety*, his secretary informs all callers that he is "on long distance to Rome."

10:00 A.M.: A screenwriter arrives to pitch a story. Marvin listens but his face betrays no reaction. He makes a point of picking up the phone during the session. He tells the writer that he is a "great talent," but has the gnawing suspicion that the writer has heard this before.

12:30 P.M.: Marvin is a half-hour late for his lunch date at Le Dôme. As he is on a first-name basis with the maître d', he gets the best table. Others wonder who he is. Marvin betrays no interest in this, but glances furtively to see if people are wondering who he is. He eats an avocado salad for lunch and drinks Perrier.

4:00 P.M.: Back in the office. Marvin goes through the day's messages but returns none of the calls.

5:00 P.M.: Marvin sees his shrink, whose office is in Beverly Hills. Marvin tells him about his meeting with the writer and wonders why he always treats writers so shabbily. The shrink tells him he is insecure. Relieved, Marvin thanks him for the insight and vows to continue treating writers shabbily now that he realizes why he does it.

6:00 P.M.: Marvin sees his psychic and asks her if his latest TV deal is going to happen. The psychic assures him that it will.

6:45 P.M.: Marvin sees his chiropractor, complaining of a twinge in his neck. The chiropractor taps a bone on Marvin's big toe and the pain disappears.

7:30 P.M. Marvin meets a young starlet at Ma Maison for a drink. She is an acquaintance of his uncle and needs a break. He promises to help her get a good agent. She thanks him profusely, and Marvin invites her for dinner the following week to, as he puts it, "discuss your career."

8:00 P.M.: Marvin drives home, undresses, and spends thirty minutes under his sun lamp. Then he relaxes for an hour in his samadhi tank. This sensory-deprivation experience causes him to think deep thoughts, such as where he should take the bimbo he just met at Ma Maison.

9:30 P.M.: Marvin reads twenty pages of a script he claimed he had read three months ago.

10:00 P.M.: Marvin goes to sleep. He always retires early so that he can rise at 5:30 the next morning to jog, sauna, work out, massage, Jacuzzi, and meditate before facing the rigors of the workday.

PART FOUR

Hollywood Babble-on

☆ ☆

The Glossary

"In two words: im possible."
—Sam Goldwyn

To most people Hollywood is an alien land with its own peculiar customs, habits, and lingo. As in any foreign country, a working knowledge of the language is essential. You would not venture to France without knowing how to ask for a toilet. Similarly, you should not venture to Hollywood without knowing how to converse with a producer. The following terms and phrases, if memorized and worked into conversation, will give others the impression that you've been around long enough to be taken seriously.

Above-the-line costs A budgetary term used to denote the fees, usually outlandish, paid to major stars, screenwriters, directors, and producers of films. In star-studded projects, above-the-line costs can be astronomical, but big names sell tickets.

Angle 1. What everyone in Hollywood has. 2. The position of the camera.

Arbitration The ultimate fate of any credit dispute, such as, "It's in arbitration at the Guild." Arbitration usually involves a script for which a director is trying to steal credit.

Below-the-line costs A budgetary term used to denote the cost of making films, generally including expenditures for crews, locations, drugs, makeup, drugs, costumes, minor costs, drugs, extras, special effects, and drugs.

157

BH The snob's abbreviation for Beverly Hills.

Bomb A film that flops at the box office.

Callback The semifinals of any audition in which an actor is asked to appear again.

Cattle call An open audition for a small part in a film or TV production held by a producer or director who wants to meet girls.

Civilian Anyone not involved in the film business.

Clout Hollywood's favorite euphemism for power.

Coke The corporation that owns Columbia Pictures.

Creative differences The most frequent reason given by a publicity department for an aborted deal. (Example: "The project has been postponed due to creative differences.") Simply put, it means the director would like to strangle the producer.

Creative input A producer's attempt to assert himself by adding irrelevancies to the script.

Critical success A term used to describe a film that has bombed at the box office.

CU The actor's favorite line in any script—the close-up.

Development An intermediate stage in filmmaking in which people are paid large sums of money to keep a film from being made.

Exhibitor A person who owns a movie theater.

Green light The term used to denote that a film project can proceed. (Example: "We got the green light from Paramount.")

Hot A common description for anyone who is rising rapidly in Hollywood's ranks. (Example: "He's a hot writer.")

Hyphenate A multi-talented soul who has the ability and the clout to perform more than one titular function on a film. (Example: writer-producer-director.)

Indie prod Independent producer.

"It'll happen" A phrase often uttered as consolation for someone who has just failed miserably. "It" refers to success.

Legs 1. A means of transportation rarely used in Hollywood and its environs due to the predominance of the automobile. 2. Box-office endurance. ("It had a great opening week, but will it have legs?")

"Let's have lunch" Hollywoodese for good riddance.

Line producer Someone hired by a film producer to oversee the administration of a production while he stays home and makes deals by the pool. Line producers do all the work but generally make less money than regular producers. Also called "hands-on producer."

Lines 1. What actors deliver in a film and tamper with in a script. 2. Long, usually thin strands of a narcotic substance used during parties, meetings, or shoots to keep the participants from becoming too laid-back.

Miniseries A long TV movie shown over several days, usually on some epic subject that could easily have been edited down to two hours. See MOW.

Mogul 1. A bump in a ski run. 2. A term used by non-Hollywoodians to denote an industry wheeler-dealer.

MOW Movie of the week. A two-hour, made-for-TV film, usually on a subject involving rape or child abuse.

Multi-pic-pac A multiple picture package. Successful writers, directors, producers, or stars are sometimes offered these as an inducement to remain at one studio. Generally, they are cut short when the second project is a bomb (which it invariably is).

Novelization A relatively new form of literature in which a work of prose fiction is written from a film script.

OPM Other peoples' money. (i.e., what one prefers to use to finance a film project).

Option Usually a year's

lease on a piece of writing. During this period the optioner has the right to treat the optionee like an indentured servant.

Package The practice of getting big names to commit to a script in order to keep studio execs from having to do their jobs.

Pay-or-play A contract clause ensuring that an actor will be paid his full fee even if the film project in question falls apart.

Pitch A verbal spiel containing the important plot and character elements of a proposed film script or teleplay. The writer's sales pitch.

Points Hollywood's quaint version of profit sharing; a percentage of a film's profits offered to actors, writers, producers, and directors, but rarely paid.

Polish The final rewrite on a script, generally performed by someone other than the original author.

Pre-pro Pre-production; the stage of filmmaking in which the participants prepare for production.

Prequel A sequel in which the action of the film takes place prior to the time frame of the original. (Example: *Butch and Sundance—The Early Years*. The only thing that necessitated this prequel was the unfortunate fact that the producers of the original were shortsighted enough to kill off the protagonists in the original.)

Publicity flack A person hired to manipulate the press.

R rating An MPAA rating most studios strive for in order to attract minors who, by law, are not allowed to attend.

Relationship In Hollywood any romantic liaison that lasts for more than twenty minutes.

Residuals Royalties paid to participants in a TV project.

Rewrite What generally happens to a script when more than one ego becomes involved. The more egos, the more rewrites.

SAG Screen Actors Guild.

Script doctor A writer hired for an exorbitant amount of money to work a miracle cure on an ailing screenplay on which too much money has already been lavished.

Sequel A follow-up to a successful film; Hollywood's favorite way of capitalizing on success with minimum creative effort.

Sneak 1. A good description of anyone involved in the motion picture business. 2. A preview of a soon-to-be-released film in which viewers are asked to fill out questionnaires regarding their responses. When the results are negative, the film generally ends up opening in "selected theaters."

Story conference A meeting between participants of a film project in which the plotline is changed by vote.

Talent A term used exclusively to describe actors without reference to skill.

Topline To star in; to have one's credit line near the top.

Trailer 1. A movable studio office relegated to those with too little clout to merit a permanent one. 2. A short, filmed synopsis of a soon-to-be-released motion picture shown in theaters and on TV as an advertising tool to lure in audiences. Usually fast-paced and quick-edited, trailers are meant to contain only the film's high points. More often than not, the trailer is better than the film itself.

Turnaround A term used to describe a film project that is being abandoned by the studio that originally spawned it.

WGA Writers Guild of America.

. . . And More Goldwynisms

"Anybody who goes to see a psychiatrist ought to have his head examined."

"I have been laid up with intentional flu."

"He treats me like the dirt under my feet."

"I want to make a picture about the Russian secret police—the GOP."

"There is a statue of limitation."

"I read part of it all the way through."

"I had a monumental idea this morning but I didn't like it."

"I never put on a pair of shoes until I've worn them at least five years."

"Our comedies are not to be laughed at."

"Gentlemen, include me out."

"Every Tom, Dick, and Harry is named Sam."

"This makes me so sore it gets my dandruff up."

"If I could drop dead right now I'd be the happiest man alive."

A Yiddish Primer

Although the new Hollywood has little use for Yiddish, there are still enough powerful *alter kockers* around from the old Hollywood to make a cursory knowledge of the language advisable. After all, if you're at an audition or pitch session and one ancient producer turns to your agent in the middle of your spiel and refers to you as a *pisher* or *fonfer*, you'd better know what he means.

Alter kocker Old fuddy-duddy

Bluffer A person who hypes too much.

Bubbe-mayseh A bunch of malarky.

Bulba A social boo-boo.

Chozzerai Something lousy.

Cockamamie Mixed up.

Draykup A person who can talk you into something by befuddling you.

Farblondzhet Confused.

Fonfer A double-talker.

Gebenshter Talented.

Gelt Money.

Gonif A thief.

Hak a chainik To speak nonsense.

K'nacker A show-off.

Macher A big operator.

Mavin An expert.

Mezuma Money.

Megillah Anything that is boring or overdone.

Meshugge Crazy.

Naar A buffoon.

Nuchshlepper A fawning person; a sycophant.

Nudnik A nuisance or bore.

Pisher A nobody.

Platke-macher A gossip-monger.

Putz A loser.

Schlimazel A loser.

Schnorrer A bum.

Vitz A joke.

Nicknames for "The Coast"

Hollyweird
La-La Land
Lotus Land
The Big Orange
The City of Angles
Tinseltown

PART FIVE

Dealing with Success

(Globe)

☆ ☆

Just Rewards

Now that we have thoroughly discussed the ways and means of making it in Hollywood, it is time to talk about the rewards in store for those who have achieved some measure of success. These rewards, which can be prodigious, are divided into four basic categories: money, revenge, strokes, and social prestige.

Money Financially speaking, making it in Hollywood can mean big money. After all, anyone with enough endurance to put up with the countless humiliations involved in the climb to success ought to be well compensated. In terms of actual amounts, the sky is the limit. Actors who hit the big time can easily get a cool million for several painless days of work on a motion picture and at least half that amount for even less work on a television commercial. Well-

known screenwriters can begin to rake in six-figure deals and five-figure residuals. Producers and directors can demand high fees and numerous gross points. Agents start getting 10 percent of serious figures. Studio execs, aside from handsome salaries, can expect bonuses and attractive stock options for their labors. Generally speaking, everyone surrounding a success can get rich by osmosis.

Revenge Perhaps the sweetest aspect of success is the ability to pay back everyone who was rude or indifferent toward you during your rugged climb up the ladder. In Hollywood, this generally includes everyone you took a meeting with or did lunch with during your ascent. Now it is your turn to let that agent leave twenty messages with *your* secretary, your turn to rudely interrupt producers in the middle of *their* pitch, your turn to cut people off at cocktail parties. Just making it in Hollywood is perhaps the best revenge, but dealing out a little counter-humiliation can be enjoyable as well. People expect it in Hollywood.

Strokes Success in Hollywood means that it is all right to let your ego run amok. You can be obnoxious, petulant, moody, belligerent, rude, selfish, and thoughtless and get away with it! If this conduct causes difficulties, it will be the task of your agent and your public relations flack to smooth the ruffled feathers. Producers will fulfill your every whim and directors will coddle you. Studio execs will grovel at your feet. Everyone will stroke you. The disposition of your ego will suddenly become a number-one priority.

Social Prestige Success will suddenly thrust you into center stage of what passes for Hollywood society. You will be asked to appear at benefits, teach filmmaking courses at UCLA and expound on political subjects. Relatives and forgotten acquaintances will suddenly appear out of the woodwork to pester you, much as you pestered others when you were climbing the ladder. Maître d's will start making a concerted effort to remember your name, and members of the opposite sex will cling to you like barnacles. You will attend gala premieres; Army Archerd will interview you as you enter the Academy Award ceremonies; your birthday will be commemorated in Hank Grant's column; and you will be asked to reveal every boring detail of your private life to Barbara Walters.

The Oscar Campaign

Hollywoodians, in a sense, are pagan idol worshippers. The prevailing Hollywood Baal (not to be confused with Hollywood Bowl) is, of course, the Oscar. There are plenty of other awards available—Hollywood loves to give itself awards—but the Oscar is still *número uno* in the crowded award arena. This is true for one reason—the Oscar means big money.

Getting an Oscar means you can suddenly increase your acting, writing, directing, or producing fees. Moreover, it means your Oscar-winning film will be re-released in spring, thus bringing you more points, fame, and free publicity. An Oscar can't be beat in terms of the money it can generate.

But how does one obtain an Oscar? Simple. One campaigns for it. This is common practice in Hollywood and is wholly acceptable since it involves nothing more than an honest pursuit of fame and fortune. After all, that is what Hollywood is all about.

Campaigning is easy. First, get your publicist to grant interviews to anyone who asks. Suddenly appear at every benefit in town and out of town. Agree to do TV commercials for charitable organizations or public service announcements. Get your studio and agent to take out full-page ads in the trades. Invite members of the Academy to lunch, dinner, brunch, and parties. Commit yourself to every project you're offered. Go on *Good Morning America, The Today Show, The Tonight Show, The Merv Griffin Show,* and any local show that calls. Exposure is the key ingredient. And don't be upset if out-of-town periodicals accuse you of campaigning for the Oscar. Journalists don't vote.

The Success Game

Unfortunately, competition in Hollywood does not end with success itself—it just moves to a higher level. After all, in a town where enough is never enough, how can you tell where you stand in relation to the success of others? Are you a megasuccess, a supersuccess or simply a success? The following scoreboard may help:

AUTOMOTIVE TRANSPORTATION	POINTS
1. Chauffeured Rolls or Mercedes Limo	10
2. New Rolls or Bentley	9
3. New Mercedes 380SL	6
4. New BMW, Jag, Porsche	3
5. New Japanese or American car	1
6. Moped	0

HANGOUTS	POINTS
1. Ma Maison, Chasen's, Spago	10
2. Le Dôme, Scandia	8
3. Trumps	6
4. Ginger Man, Musso & Frank's Grill	4
5. Bob's Big Boy	0

ENTOURAGE	POINTS
1. Studio execs, entertainment lawyers, bodyguard	10
2. Stars and directors	8
3. Agents and producers	6
4. Writers	3
5. Story editors	0

ADDRESS	POINTS
1. Bel Air, Beverly Hills, Malibu	10
2. Hollywood Hills, the Canyons	8
3. Santa Monica, the Marina	6
4. Westwood	4
5. The Valley	0

EXERCISE	POINTS
1. Your own gym	10
2. Tennis and skiing (at Aspen)	8
3. Aerobics or Nautilus club	6
4. Jogging	4
5. YMCA	0

SHOPPING	POINTS
1. Gucci, Neiman-Marcus, Giorgio	10
2. Saks Fifth Avenue, Bonwit's	8
3. Camp Beverly Hills	6
4. Fred Siegel's	4
5. Sears	0

PUBLICITY	POINTS
1. Barbara Walters Special	10
2. Playboy interview	8
3. National Enquirer	6
4. Hank Grant's column	4
5. *Los Angeles Times* classified	0

CALL RETURN PERCENTAGE	POINTS
1. 100 percent within twenty minutes	10
2. 80 percent within an hour	8
3. 60 percent within two hours	6
4. 40 percent within a day	4
5. 20 percent within a week	2
6. Phone out of order due to lack of use	0

SECRETARIAL HELP   POINTS

1. Private/Male (British, with accent)............... 10
2. Office/Female (British, with accent)............. 8
3. Australian with accent............................ 6
4. American with Ph.D. in film...................... 4
5. American with B.A................................ 2
6. Kelly Girl or Temp............................... 0

HOME SECURITY   POINTS

1. Private guards and dogs 10
2. Dogs, high fence, alarm system................... 8
3. Neighborhood patrol guards...................... 6
4. Electronic alarm system 4
5. High wire fence................................... 2
6. Wraparound insurance policy..................... 0

TIMES PER WEEK YOU SEE SHRINK	POINTS
1. Five	10
2. Three	8
3. Two	5
4. One	0

PLAYROOMS	POINTS
1. Screening room, game room, sauna, gym	10
2. Game room, sauna	8
3. Gym	6
4. Sauna	4
5. Cabana	2
6. Rec room	0

NUMBER OF FAILED MARRIAGES	POINTS
1. Five	10
2. Three	8
3. Two	6
4. One	4
5. Zero	0

SCORING:

115–130:   You are a megasuccess. Congratulations. Everyone will despise you for it and secretly hope that you fall on your face. Make some smart investments.

100–114:   Not bad. You're a supersuccess, ardently chiseling away at the top. Don't trust anybody.

80–99:   A mere success, a dime a dozen in Hollywood. Keep the hype level up and you might be able to matriculate up a notch.

☆ ☆

Author's Pitch

Purely for the sake of maintaining objectivity, the author of this book has scrupulously avoided pursuing Hollywood stardom. He does not drive a Rolls or even a Mercedes, nor does he hang out at Ma Maison, Trumps, or the Polo Lounge. He doesn't have a swimming pool, Jacuzzi, private screening room, tennis court, entourage, or entertainment lawyers. He has never been to Cannes. All this has been sacrificed to ensure the integrity of this project.

One of the simplest ways of achieving Hollywood stardom, of course, is to write a book and have it optioned for television or the movies. The author does not wish anyone to think that this book was written with that in mind, but the fact is, *The Official Hollywood Handbook* is now available to producers, directors, and studio execs interested in purchasing the rights. Think of it—an eighteen-hour miniseries of epic proportions! A major motion picture in living color and Dolby sound! A cast of thousands! Special effects! Oscar-winning performances! Huge box-office grosses!

Although the material may not immediately strike you as adaptable to the screen (large or small), it can be altered. Chase scenes, blood and gore, food fights, a love story and, if there's time, even a plot can be added!

If you're a producer, director, or studio exec interested in buying rights to this book, simply fill out the following form and mail it to Simon & Schuster, 1230 Avenue of the Americas, NY 10020.

My people will call your people.

---- ☆ ----

Producer's Option Form for *The Official Hollywood Handbook*

_____ Yes, I'm high on the concept and would like to talk deal. Let's do lunch.

_____ Pass

Name: _____

Studio: _____

Position: _____

Hangouts: _____

References:

1. I'm a close personal friend of _____

2. I drive a: Rolls   Bentley   Mercedes   Porsche   Jag   BMW

Agreement:

I, _____ , solemnly swear that
        (*the undersigned*)

I will return all phone calls within twenty-four hours and never put the author on hold for more than sixty seconds. I also hereby swear that my secretary will never tell the author that I am in a meeting, in Cannes for the month, on the other line, or in conference.

_____   _____
   (*Date*)   (*Signed*)